Bite~Size
Bible®
CHARTS

RON RHODES

HARVEST HOUSE PUBLISHERS
EUGENE, OREGON

Cover by Dugan Design Group, Bloomington, Minnesota

Cover photo © Dugan Design Group

BITE-SIZE BIBLE is a registered trademark of The Hawkins Children's LLC. Harvest House Publishers, Inc. is the exclusive licensee of the federally registered trademark BITE-SIZE BIBLE.

BITE-SIZE BIBLE® CHARTS
Copyright © 2012 by Ron Rhodes
Published by Harvest House Publishers
Eugene, Oregon 97402
www.harvesthousepublishers.com

ISBN 978-0-7369-4481-6 (pbk.)
ISBN 978-0-7369-4482-3 (eBook)

Printed in the United States of America

12 13 14 15 16 17 18 19 20 / BP-SK / 10 9 8 7 6 5 4 3 2 1

To Bible students everywhere!

Acknowledgments

I am ever thankful to God for the wondrous gift of my family—Kerri, David, and Kylie. Their generous and sacrificial support of my work in ministry means the world to me. I also continue to be thankful for my ongoing relationship with the wonderful folks at Harvest House Publishers, all of whom have a sincere heart for the Lord and His truth. Most of all, I am thankful to the Lord Jesus Himself for the opportunity to serve His kingdom in a small way.

Contents

Introduction

Good things come in small packages.

I'm not sure who first coined this phrase, but I think there is some truth to it. This book is a small book—a bite-size book. But it's brimming with helpful charts on a variety of important and interesting issues.

My goal has been to produce a book that is small enough to put in a briefcase or a purse, low-cost, and yet loaded with helpful information you can really use. This book provides concise, reliable charts on diverse issues: the Bible, God, Jesus Christ, the Holy Spirit, humankind, sin, salvation, angels, demons, the prophetic future, the afterlife, prayer, Christian ethics, apologetics, and more.

You'll find these charts to be helpful learning tools as well as helpful teaching tools. I pray you will find this book to be more than a bite-size blessing!

As you go through the book, be sure to look up some of the Scripture references I cite. You will increasingly discover, as I have through the years, that the Word of God is a light that guides us (Psalm 119:105), an encourager of our souls (Psalm 119:25,37,40,50), and an anchor that keeps us steady (see Hebrews 6:19).

Free PowerPoint versions of the charts are available to those who have purchased this book. These will be especially useful for teachers and Bible study leaders. Visit bitesizebiblebooks.com, where you will find instructions for downloading the charts.

The Bible

How We Got the Bible

Inspiration

God superintended the human authors of Scripture, who used their own individual personalities and writing styles to compose and record without error His revelation to humankind.

Acceptance

The 39 Old Testament books and 27 New Testament books were written over a long period of time. Many of them were recognized as inspired when they were initially written (see, for example, 2 Peter 3:15-16).

Transmission

Before the printing press was invented, scribes made copies of individual Bible books by hand.

Canonization

Books recognized as Scripture, under God's guidance, were eventually collected and arranged by church councils based on careful guidelines.

Translation

By AD 200, the Bible had been translated into seven languages.

Duplication

Once the printing press was invented, the Bible was mass-produced in many languages.

Views of the Inspiration of Scripture

Theory	Explanation
Dictation	God raised up men, prepared their vocabularies, and then dictated Scripture to them.
Inspired concept	The Bible's concepts are inspired, but its exact words are not.
Inspired purpose	The Bible contains many factual errors, but it has doctrinal integrity and thus accomplishes God's purpose for it.
Mystical	The writers of Scripture were Spirit-filled and spirit-guided believers.
Natural inspiration	The writers of Scripture were men of great genius and natural talent. There was no supernatural process involved.
Neoorthodox	The Bible is a fallible witness that points to Christ.
Orthodox (the correct view)	God superintended human writers who used their own personalities and writing styles to record without error God's word to man.
Partial inspiration	The parts of the Bible that were otherwise unknowable were inspired.

God Speaks Through the Prophets

Spoken By...	Attributed To...
The psalmist (Psalm 95:7-11)	Holy Spirit (Hebrews 3:7-11)
The psalmist (Psalm 45:6)	God (Hebrews 1:6-8)
The psalmist (Psalm 102:25,27)	God (Hebrews 1:6,10-12)
Isaiah (Isaiah 7:14)	The Lord (Matthew 1:22-23)
Hosea (Hosea 11:1)	The Lord (Matthew 2:15)
Eliphaz (Job 5:13)	God (1 Corinthians 3:19)

All Scripture Is Inspired

Biblical Authors	References to Inspiration
Moses	Joshua 1:7; 1 Kings 2:3; 2 Kings 14:6; 2 Chronicles 17:9
The later prophets	Jeremiah 26:18; Ezekiel 14:14,20; Daniel 9:2
Luke	1 Timothy 5:18 (compare with Deuteronomy 25:4 and Luke 10:7)
The apostle Paul	2 Peter 3:15-16
All Scripture writers	2 Timothy 3:16

Early New Testament Manuscripts

Manuscript	Date	Biblical Books
Chester Beatty Papyrus 45	Third century	All four Gospels and Acts 4–17
Chester Beatty Papyrus 46	AD 200	Ten Pauline epistles and the book of Hebrews
Chester Beatty Papyrus 47	Third century	Revelation 9:10–17:2
Bodmer Papyrus 66	AD 200	The Gospel of John
Bodmer Papyrus 75	Third century	Luke and John
Sinaiticus Uncial	Fourth century	The entire New Testament
Vaticanus Uncial	Fourth century	Most of the New Testament
Washingtonianus Uncial	Early fifth century	All four Gospels
Alexandrinus Uncial	Fifth century	Most of the New Testament
Ephraemi Rescriptus Uncial	Fifth century	Portions of every New Testament book except 2 Thessalonians and 2 John

Five Tests for Canonicity

At the Council of Carthage (AD 397), the church formally recognized which books belonged in the canon. Five primary tests guided them.

Test	Explanation
Was the book written or backed by a prophet or apostle of God?	The Word of God, inspired by the Spirit of God for the people of God, must be communicated through a man of God (Deuteronomy 18:18; 2 Peter 1:20-21).
Is the book authoritative?	Does the book ring with the sense of "Thus saith the Lord"?
Does the book tell the truth about God?	The Bereans searched the Old Testament Scriptures to verify Paul's teaching (Acts 17:11). They knew that agreement with all earlier revelation is essential.
Does the book give evidence of having the power of God?	Any writing that does not exhibit God's transforming power in the lives of its readers could not have come from God (Hebrews 4:12).
Was the book accepted by the people of God?	It is the norm that God's people initially receive God's Word (see 1 Thessalonians 2:13).

Hebrew Classification of Old Testament Books

Torah
Genesis, Exodus, Leviticus, Numbers, Deuteronomy

Former Prophets
Joshua, Judges, 1 Samuel, 2 Samuel, 1 Kings, 2 Kings

Latter Prophets
Isaiah, Jeremiah, Ezekiel, Hosea, Joel, Amos, Obadiah, Jonah, Micah, Nahum, Habakkuk, Zephaniah, Haggai, Zechariah, Malachi

Writings
Ruth, 1 Chronicles, 2 Chronicles, Ezra, Nehemiah, Esther, Job, Psalms, Proverbs, Ecclesiastes, Song of Solomon, Lamentations, Daniel

Classification of New Testament Books

Biographical—Matthew, Mark, Luke, John

Historical—Acts

Pauline Epistles
Romans, 1 Corinthians, 2 Corinthians, Galatians, Ephesians, Philippians, Colossians, 1 Thessalonians, 2 Thessalonians, 1 Timothy, 2 Timothy, Titus, Philemon

General Epistles
Hebrews, James, 1 Peter, 2 Peter, 1 John, 2 John, 3 John, Jude

Apocalyptic—Revelation

Rightly Interpreting the Bible

Author's meaning	Seek the author's intended meaning instead of superimposing a meaning onto the text.
Context	Interpret each verse in context. Every word is part of a verse, every verse is part of a paragraph, every paragraph is part of a book, and every book is part of the whole of Scripture.
History	Consult other books to get a better grasp of the historical context of the biblical book.
Genre	Make a correct genre judgment. Biblical genres include history (Acts), dramatic epics (Job), poetry (Psalms), wise sayings (Proverbs), and apocalyptic writings (Revelation). Poetry should not be interpreted as history!
The New Testament	Interpret the Old Testament according to the greater light of the New Testament.
Clear verses	Interpret the more difficult verses in light of the clearer verses.
The Holy Spirit	Depend on the Holy Spirit for guidance (John 16:12-15; 1 Corinthians 2:9-11).

The Formal Equivalence Approach to Bible Translation

Definition

The formal equivalence approach advocates as literal a rendering of the original text as possible. The translator attempts to render the exact words from Hebrew, Aramaic, and Greek into English. This is why the word "formal" is used—the rendering is form-for-form or word-for-word.

Example

New American Standard Bible (NASB).

Style

Literal translations help retain the writing style of the original writers.

Beauty and Terminology

Literal translations better preserve the original beauty of Scripture and retain important theological terminology, such as "justification."

Commentary

Literal translations can be trusted not to mix too much commentary into the text.

The Dynamic Equivalence Approach to Bible Translation

Definition

The dynamic equivalence approach advocates a readable translation that does not provide an exact rendering of the original languages. It is a thought-for-thought, meaning-driven translation. It seeks to produce the same dynamic impact on modern readers the original had upon its audience.

Readability

Dynamic equivalence translations generally use shorter words, shorter sentences, and shorter paragraphs.

Terminology

Such translations use basic vocabulary and easy-to-understand substitutes for theological terminology.

Contemporary

Culturally dependent phraseology (such as "Thus saith the Lord") is converted into more contemporary language ("The Lord says").

More Natural

The word order of the original Hebrew and Greek may be altered to produce a more natural English reading.

Gender-Inclusive Language in Bible Translations

Advantages	Disadvantages
It more clearly and accurately conveys the author's intended meaning.	Such translations could lose elegance by overusing such words as "people" and "persons."
Some grammatical guides allow the use of "they" and "them" in place of "he" and "him."	Changing singular references to "they" or "them" could obscure God's personal dealings with individuals.
Gender-sensitive language does not change the essential meaning of the text.	Such translations are not as faithful to the original languages.
The Bible was written for people of both genders, so "brothers" is better rendered "brothers and sisters."	God Himself chose the words of Scripture, and translators do not have the prerogative to change them.
Many female readers of the Bible feel left out by exclusively male terminology.	Patriarchalism was part of the biblical culture, and to obscure it by removing male-oriented language could lead people astray from this aspect of the Bible.

2

Bible Backgrounds

Key Prophets of the Old Testament

Prophet	Date	Target Audience
Elijah	870–845 BC	Israel
Elisha	845–800 BC	Israel
Jonah	About 781 BC	Nineveh
Isaiah	760–673 BC	Judah
Hosea	758–725 BC	Israel
Micah	738–698 BC	Judah
Jeremiah	650–582 BC	Judah
Ezekiel	620–570 BC	Exiles in Babylon
Daniel	620–540 BC	Exiles in Babylon
Habakkuk	608–598 BC	Judah
Obadiah	About 590 BC	About Edom
Zechariah	522–509 BC	Judah
Haggai	About 520 BC	Judah
Malachi	About 465 BC	Judah
Joel	About 450 BC	Judah

The Biblical Covenants

Definition   A covenant is an agreement between two parties. Covenants were used among the ancients as…

- treaties or alliances between nations (1 Samuel 11:1)
- treaties between individual people (Genesis 21:27)
- friendship pacts (1 Samuel 18:3-4)
- agreements between God and His people (see below)

Abrahamic Covenant

God made a covenant with Abraham (Genesis 12:1-3) and reaffirmed it with Isaac (17:21) and Jacob (35:10-12). It included these promises:

- I will make you a great nation.
- I will give you and your descendants a rich land that will remain your possession forever.
- I will bless you.
- I will make your name great.
- You will be a blessing.
- I will bless those who bless you and curse those who curse you.
- All peoples on earth will be blessed through you.

Mosaic Covenant	God made a covenant with Israel at Mount Sinai following Israel's deliverance from Egypt. This covenant constituted the formal basis of the redemptive relationship between God and the Israelites (Exodus 19:3-25). God gave the law—stipulations to the people explaining their responsibilities (Exodus 20:1-17). He promised blessing for obedience and judgment for disobedience (Deuteronomy 29–30).
Davidic Covenant	God promised David that one of his descendants would rule forever (2 Samuel 7:12-13; 22:51). This covenant finds its ultimate fulfillment in Jesus Christ, who was born from the line of David (Matthew 1:1).
New Covenant	This covenant promised forgiveness of sin, based entirely on the sacrificial death and resurrection of Christ (Jeremiah 31:31-34). When Christ ate the Passover meal with the disciples in the Upper Room, He said, "This cup is the new covenant in my blood" (Luke 22:20; see also 1 Corinthians 11:25).

Jewish Feasts

Passover	The evening before the fourteenth of Nissan, the Jews celebrated their escape from Egypt under Moses' leadership (see Exodus 12:3-11). Each family sacrificed a lamb to commemorate the sacrifice that took place prior to the exodus.
Unleavened Bread	During the Passover meal and throughout the following week, the Israelites ate unleavened bread (Exodus 23:15). It was made without yeast and was prepared very quickly. This reminded the Israelites of the hurried preparations they made when Pharaoh finally allowed them to leave Egypt.
Harvest (or Weeks)	This feast was held in the spring at the beginning of the wheat harvest (Exodus 23:16; 34:22). Two loaves made of new grain were presented to the Lord (Leviticus 23:15-21). In this way, the people gave thanks to God for the grain He provided them.
Ingathering	This feast was held in early autumn (September–October) at the end of the agricultural year (Exodus 23:16). It was a time of thanksgiving for the final harvest God provided.

The Day of Atonement	On this day, all Israelites confessed their sins to God and asked His forgiveness and cleansing (Leviticus 16). The high priest offered a sacrifice for his own sins and then offered a sacrifice on behalf of the people.
Purim	"Purim" literally means "lots" and refers to the lots that were cast by the chief minister of King Ahasuerus to decide which day he should massacre the Jews. The Lord saved them (Esther 9:23-32).
Hanukkah	On this holy day, Jews commemorate the cleansing and rededication of the temple by Judas Maccabaeus in 164 BC.

Jewish Offerings

Sin Offering	This offering was presented for ritual cleansing, for unintentional sins against God, and for the Hebrew festivals (including the Day of Atonement). It included a sacrifice (see Leviticus 4:5-13) to cleanse the defilement caused by sin.
Guilt Offering	This offering made restitution when social, religious, or ritual expectations had not been observed. Guilt was vicariously transferred to the sacrificial animal through laying hands on it.
Burnt Offering	This offering symbolized the worshipper's homage and total dedication to God. An animal (in perfect condition) was sacrificed whole (Leviticus 6:22). The worshipper placed his hands on the sacrificial animal as an indication that the animal was being sacrificed for the worshipper's own failings.
Cereal Offering or Meal Offering	This goodwill offering to God expressed homage and thankfulness to Him.
Drink Offering	A liquid (such as wine—Exodus 29:40) was offered daily and again on the Sabbath, new moon, and annual festivals. It was intended to bring pleasure to God.

Peace Offering	This offering was intended to express the desire to maintain right relations between God, man, and neighbor. The fat of the animal (considered the best portion of the animal) was burnt on the altar. The meat was then eaten by the worshippers and their families (see Deuteronomy 12:18).
Voluntary Offering	This offering was considered an appropriate response to the goodness of God. Because it was voluntary, an imperfectly developed ox or sheep was acceptable.

Jewish Sects of the First Century

Pharisees	Pharisees constituted a religious and political party in Palestine. They were religious purists who preserved and obeyed the law and forcefully encouraged others to do the same. Jesus experienced Pharisaic opposition to His ministry (Matthew 15:1-12). He chastised them for being more committed to external observances than to true inner purity (Matthew 6:2,5,16; 23:5-7).
Sadducees	Sadducees typically came from wealthy families. Most of the chief priests in New Testament times were Sadducees. They were dominant in the Sanhedrin. They believed only in the Torah and denied the existence of angels, the resurrection, and the immortality of the soul. They opposed Jesus (Matthew 22:23-33). Jesus warned His followers of the "leaven" of the Sadducees (Matthew 16:1-12).
Scribes	Scribes copied and recopied portions of Scripture for 1500 years of biblical history. Eventually they became the official interpreters of the law. In New Testament times they were often called "lawyers," pointing to their role as experts in the Mosaic law (Matthew 22:35). Jesus warned His followers about the hypocrisy of the scribes (Matthew 23).

Zealots	Zealots were fanatical Jewish patriots who believed that the Jews should not be subject to any foreign power, such as the Romans (Matthew 10:4).
Samaritans	Samaritans were considered racially impure and unclean by mainstream Jews. Some Israelites from the tribes of Ephraim and Manasseh intermarried with Assyrians following the fall of Samaria in 722 BC.

The Twelve Apostles

Peter	One of the "inner three" who saw some of Jesus' greatest miracles and witnessed Jesus in His true glory (2 Peter 1:16-18).
Andrew	The brother of Simon Peter (Matthew 4:18; 10:2) who resided in Bethsaida in Galilee (John 1:44). He was present at some of Christ's most incredible miracles.
James	The brother of John who was present at the transfiguration and in Gethsemane (Matthew 4:21; 10:2; 17:1).
John	James' brother and Peter's fishing partner. He was present at the transfiguration and in Gethsemane. He was "the disciple whom Jesus loved" and became a leader in the Jerusalem church (Matthew 4:21; 10:2).
Philip	A native of Bethsaida who introduced Nathaniel to Jesus (Matthew 10:3; John 1:45-51).
Bartholomew	Also called Nathanael in John 1:45-51. Bartholomew was among the disciples the risen Lord appeared to at the Sea of Tiberias (John 21:2). He also witnessed the ascension (Acts 1:4,12-13).

Thomas	Also called Didymus (John 11:16), Thomas became widely known as "doubting Thomas" for his initial skepticism about Christ's resurrection (John 20:24-28). But he quickly became convinced.
Matthew	A tax collector also known as Levi, he was the son of Alphaeus (Matthew 9:9; 10:3).
James	A son of Alphaeus and Mary, this James was known as "the small" or "the younger" (Matthew 10:3; 27:56; Mark 3:18; 15:40).
Judas	Not to be confused with Iscariot, this Judas was the son of James. He was also called Thaddaeus. He may have been a zealot (Matthew 10:3; Mark 3:18; Luke 6:16).
Simon the Zealot	A disciple apparently martyred with Jude in Persia (see Matthew 10:4; Mark 3:18).
Judas Iscariot	The betrayer of Christ and "son of perdition." He had been the treasurer of the disciples who traveled with Jesus (Matthew 10:4; 26:14-50; Mark 3:19; 14:10; Luke 6:16).

Types of Parables in the New Testament

Similes

These parables involve a likeness and use the words "like" or "as."

Example: Jesus said, "I am sending you out like sheep among wolves" (Matthew 10:16).

Metaphors

These parables involve an implied likeness.

Example: Jesus said, "I am the gate for the sheep" (John 10:7). This metaphor teaches that Jesus is the way of salvation.

Similitudes

In these parables, Jesus uses a familiar aspect of the natural world as a word picture to illustrate a spiritual truth.

Example: In Matthew 13:33, Jesus compared the kingdom of God to yeast, thereby demonstrating the penetrating power of the gospel.

Stories

Jesus also told stories to illustrate spiritual truth.

Example: In Luke 15:11-32 Jesus told a story of the prodigal son to illustrate God's love for repentant sinners.

The Apostle Paul's Missionary Journeys

First missionary journey	Travelers: Paul, Barnabas, and John Mark
	Date: AD 47–49
	Main route: Cyprus and Turkey
	Distance: 1400 miles
	Scripture: Acts 13–14
Second missionary journey	Travelers: Paul, Silas, Timothy, Priscilla, Aquilla, and Luke
	Date: AD 49–51
	Main route: Syria, Turkey, Greece, and Jerusalem
	Distance: 2800 miles
	Scripture: Acts 15:36–18:22
Third missionary journey	Travelers: Paul, Timothy, Luke, and others
	Date: AD 52–57
	Main route: Turkey, Greece, Lebanon, and Israel
	Distance: 2700 miles
	Scripture: Acts 18:23–21:16

3

God

Arguments for the Existence of God

Cosmological	Every effect must have an adequate cause. The universe is an effect, so it must have a cause. Reason demands that whatever caused the universe must be greater than the universe. That cause is God (who Himself is the uncaused First Cause). "Every house is built by someone, but God is the builder of everything" (Hebrews 3:4).
Teleological	The earth and universe exhibit an obvious purposeful and intricate design. If one found a watch in the sand, the assumption would be that someone created the watch because its various parts couldn't have jumped together to create its intricate design. Similarly, the perfect design of the universe points to a Designer, and that Designer is God.

Ontological	Most human beings have an innate idea of a most perfect being. Where did this idea come from? A perfect being (God) must have planted the idea in human minds. If God did not exist, one could conceive of an even greater being that did exist. Thus God must in fact exist.
Moral	Every human being has an innate sense of moral obligation. Where did this sense of "oughtness" come from? The source must be God. The existence of a moral law in the human heart demands the existence of a moral lawgiver (see Romans 1:19-32).
Anthropological	Human beings have personality (mind, emotions, and will). Personal beings cannot come from an impersonal source, so a personal cause must exist—God (see Genesis 1:26-27).

God Is a Person

Definition of a person	A person is a conscious being who thinks, feels, purposes, and carries these purposes into action. A person engages in active relationships with others. God does all this!
Abba	The Bible pictures God as a loving personal Father to whom believers may cry, "Abba" (Romans 8:15), a term meaning "daddy."
Father	Jesus often spoke of God as a loving Father. The apostle Paul referred to God as a "Father of compassion" (2 Corinthians 1:3).

God Is a Spirit

Scripture	"God is spirit" (John 4:24).
Not physical	Jesus affirmed that a spirit does not have flesh and bones (Luke 24:39). God is not a physical being.
Not visible	God is "the King eternal, immortal, invisible, the only God" (1 Timothy 1:17).
No body parts	References in Scripture to God's face, ears, eyes, hands, and strong arm are humanlike terms that help us understand God better.

The Trinity

Definition

There is one God, and in the unity of the godhead are three coequal and coeternal persons: Father, Son, and Holy Spirit. This doctrine is based on the following three lines of biblical evidence.

There is one God.	God's oneness is the uniform testimony of the Bible (Isaiah 44:6; 46:9; John 5:44; 17:3; Romans 3:29-30; 16:27; Ephesians 4:6; 1 Timothy 2:5; James 2:19).
Three persons are called God.	The Father (1 Peter 1:2)
	Jesus (Hebrews 1:8)
	The Holy Spirit (Acts 5:3-4)
The godhead is three in one.	Baptism is in the name of the Father, the Son, and the Holy Spirit (Matthew 28:19). "Name" is singular in the Greek, indicating one God. The definite articles before "Father," "Son," and "Holy Spirit" indicate distinct persons (see also 2 Corinthians 13:14).

The Names of God

Name	Meaning
Yahweh	"I AM." God is eternally self-existent (see Exodus 3:14-15).
Yahweh Nissi	"The LORD is my Banner." Israel could not defeat its enemies alone. The battles were to be the Lord's because He was Israel's banner—its source of victory (Exodus 17:15).
Yahweh Rapha	"The LORD, who heals you" (Exodus 15:26).
Yahweh Nakeh	"The LORD who strikes you." Yahweh disciplines His people (Ezekiel 7:9).
Yahweh El Gemolah	"The LORD is a God of retribution" (Jeremiah 51:56).
Yahweh Raah	"The LORD is my shepherd" (Psalm 23:1).
Yahweh Tsidkenu	"The LORD Our Righteous Savior" (Jeremiah 23:6). God is righteous and brings righteousness to His people.
Yahweh Maccaddeshem	"The LORD, who makes you holy." Yahweh sanctifies His people (Exodus 31:13).

Name	Meaning
Yahweh Shammah	"The LORD is there." Yahweh is always present with His people (Ezekiel 48:35).
Elohim	"Strong One" or "Mighty One" (Genesis 1:1).
El Shaddai	"El" in Hebrew refers to "Mighty God" (see Genesis 17:1-20). "Shaddai" is derived from a root word that refers to a mother's breast. God is mighty, but He is also compassionate, like a mother.
El Roi	"The God who sees me" (Genesis 16:13).
El Olam	"The Eternal God" (Genesis 21:33; Isaiah 40:28).
Adonai	Lord and Master (Genesis 18:27).
Lord of Hosts	The sovereign commander of a great heavenly army of angels (Psalm 89:8; see 91:11-12).

Modalism Is False

Definition
Modalism views the Father, Son, and Holy Spirit not as persons but as modes of manifestation of the one God.

Three distinct persons	The error of modalism is evident in that all three persons in the New Testament are portrayed together (Matthew 28:19; 2 Corinthians 13:14).
The Father and Son are distinct	The Father sent the son (John 3:17). The Father and Son love each other (John 14:31). The Father speaks to the Son, and the Son speaks to the Father (John 11:41-42).
Jesus and the Holy Spirit are distinct	The Holy Spirit comes upon Jesus at the baptism (Matthew 3:16). The Holy Spirit glorifies Jesus and reminds us of His teachings (John 16:12-15). Jesus and the Father sent the Holy Spirit (John 15:26).

Conclusion
Clearly, the Father, Son, and Holy Spirit are distinct persons who interact with each other within the unity of the one godhead.

God's Attributes Reveal His Nature

Eternal	God has always existed (Psalm 90:2; Revelation 1:8).
Loving	God is the very personification of love (1 John 4:8,16). Love permeates His being.
Everywhere-present	There is nowhere one can go where God is not (Psalm 139:7-12; Jeremiah 23:23-24).
All-knowing	God knows all things, both actual and possible (Matthew 11:21-23). He knows all things past (Isaiah 41:22), present (Hebrews 4:13), and future (Isaiah 46:10).
All-powerful	God's power is limitless (Genesis 18:14; Psalm 147:5; Jeremiah 32:17,27).
Sovereign	God rules the universe, controls all things, and is Lord over all (Psalm 50:1; 66:7; 93:1).
Holy	God is entirely separate from all evil and is pure in every way (Exodus 15:11; Leviticus 19:2; Psalm 71:22; Isaiah 6:3).
Immutable	God's essential nature is unchanging and unchangeable (Psalm 102:25-27; Malachi 3:6).

Pantheism Is False

Definition

Pantheism is the view that all is God and God is all.

No distinctions	In this view, all distinctions between creation (finite) and the Creator (infinite) are erased. But biblically, God is eternally distinct from what He created (Hebrews 11:3; see also Genesis 1:1; Psalm 33:8-9).
Violates common sense	Pantheism contradicts common sense. If all is truly God, then there is no difference between myself and anything else in the world.
Existence of evil	Pantheism fails to adequately deal with the existence of evil in the world. If all is God, then both good and evil stem from one and the same essence (God). This view forces one to say that Hitler and his regime were part of God.
Impersonal	The pantheistic God is impersonal, not a personal being with whom relationships can be established (see Mark 14:36).

Polytheism Is False

Definition

Polytheism is the view that there are many gods. This view is held by Mormons, New Agers, and neo-pagans.

The biblical testimony	The fact that there is only one true God is the consistent testimony of Scripture from Genesis to Revelation (see John 5:44; 17:3; Romans 3:29-30; 16:27; Galatians 3:20; Ephesians 4:5-6; 1 Timothy 2:5; James 2:19).
God's own affirmations	"I am the first and I am the last; apart from me there is no God" (Isaiah 44:6). "I am God, and there is no other; I am God, and there is none like me" (Isaiah 46:9). See also Deuteronomy 6:4; 32:39; 2 Samuel 7:22; Isaiah 37:20; 43:10; 45:5,14,21-22.

Conclusion

There are many false gods, but there is only one true God (1 Corinthians 8:4-6).

The Ten Plagues and Egypt's False Gods

Plague	False Gods Judged
1. The Nile turned to blood (Exodus 7:17)	Nilus was the Egyptian river god.
2. Frogs (Exodus 8:1-15)	The goddess Heqt was made in the image of a frog.
3. Gnats (Exodus 8:16-19)	The gnats would have rendered the Egyptian priests ritually unclean. This may have also been a judgment against Geb, god of the earth, because the dust turned into gnats.
4. Flies (Exodus 8:20-32)	This was apparently directed at Khepri, who had the head of a fly.
5. A plague on livestock (Exodus 9:1-7)	Hathor, mother and sky goddess, took the form of a cow. Apis, who symbolized fertility, took the form of a bull.
6. Boils and sores (Exodus 9:8-12)	The Egyptian deity Sekhmet, a lion-headed goddess, was considered to have the power of bringing epidemics to an end.

Plague	False Gods Judged
7. Hail (Exodus 9:13-35)	This judgment was directed against Shu, the Egyptian god of the atmosphere, and Osiris, who sometimes functioned as a god of agriculture.
8. Locusts (Exodus 10:1-20)	This was directed against Serapis, the Egyptian god who was supposedly able to protect the land from locusts.
9. Darkness (Exodus 10:21-22)	This judgment was against the Egyptian sun god, Re. The gods Aten and Atum were also shown to be powerless.
10. The firstborn of all the land died (Exodus 11:1–12:36).	This was apparently a judgment against Pharaoh, considered to be the son of god.

4

Jesus Christ

The Angel of the Lord: The Preincarnate Christ

Activity or Attribute	Angel of the Lord	Jesus Christ
Both are called Lord.	Genesis 16:7,13	John 20:28
Both are called God.	Genesis 48:15-16	Hebrews 1:8
Both claimed to be "I AM."	Exodus 3:2,5-6,14	John 8:58
Both are named wonderful.	Judges 13:15,18	Isaiah 9:6
Both are sent from God (the Father).	Exodus 23:20	John 5:30; 6:38
Both guide God's people.	Exodus 14:19	Matthew 28:20
Both loved and redeemed people.	Isaiah 63:9	Ephesians 5:25
Both command the Lord's army.	Joshua 5:13-15	Revelation 19:11-14

Messianic Prophecies Fulfilled by Jesus Christ

Topic	Old Testament Prophecy	New Testament Fulfillment
Line of Abraham	Genesis 12:2	Matthew 1:1
Line of David	2 Samuel 7:12-16	Matthew 1:1
Virgin birth	Isaiah 7:14	Matthew 1:23
Born in Bethlehem	Micah 5:2	Matthew 2:6
Escape into Egypt	Hosea 11:1	Matthew 2:14
Named Immanuel	Isaiah 7:14	Matthew 1:23
Forsaken by God	Psalm 22:1	Matthew 27:46
Forsaken by others	Zechariah 13:7	Mark 14:50
Silent	Isaiah 53:7	Matthew 27:12-19
Hands and feet pierced	Psalm 22:16	John 20:25
No bones broken	Psalm 22:17	John 19:33-36
Offered vinegar	Psalm 69:21	Matthew 27:34
Scourged and killed	Isaiah 53:5	John 19:1,18
Resurrected	Psalm 16:10	Matthew 28:6
Ascended	Psalm 68:18	Luke 24:50-53

Old Testament Types of Christ

A type is an Old Testament institution, event, person, or object that has reality and purpose in biblical history but also by divine design foreshadows something yet to be revealed. Many Old Testament persons are types of Christ.

Aaron	Aaron was appointed to his sacred office; Christ was appointed to His (Hebrews 5:4-6). Aaron was an earthly high priest; Christ is the heavenly high priest (Hebrews 8:1-5). Aaron administered the old covenant; Christ ministered the new (verse 6). Aaron offered sacrifices daily; Christ offered Himself once for all (Hebrews 7:27).
David	As a shepherd, David led and cared for his sheep. As a king, he ruled in power and sovereignty over his people. Christ is the ultimate Shepherd and King.
Joseph	Both Joseph and Christ were born by a special intervention of God (Genesis 30:22-24; Luke 1:35), loved by their fathers, hated by their brethren, and conspired against (Genesis 37:3-4,28; Matthew 26:3-4; John 3:35; 15:24-25). Both were sold for silver (Genesis 37:28; Matthew 26:14-15), condemned though innocent (Genesis 39:11-20; Matthew 27:19,24), and raised to glory by God (Genesis 45:16-18; Isaiah 65:17-25).

Melchizedek	Melchizedek's name is made up of two words meaning "king" and "righteous." Melchizedek was also a priest. Thus, Melchizedek foreshadows Christ as a righteous King-Priest. Melchizedek was the king of Salem, a word that means peace. This points to Christ as the King of peace.
Moses	Both Moses and Jesus were endangered as little children (Exodus 1:22; Matthew 2:13) and rejected by their brethren (Exodus 2:11-15; John 1:11; Acts 7:25-29). Both were deliverers of God's people (Exodus 3:7-10), prophets (Deuteronomy 18:15; Matthew 13:57; John 12:29), intercessors (Exodus 17:1-6; Hebrews 7:25), and rulers (Deuteronomy 33:4-5; John 1:49).

Jesus Is God

Comparison of Old Testament and New Testament	Only God is Creator (Isaiah 44:24), yet the New Testament calls Jesus Creator (John 1:3; Colossians 1:16). Only God is Savior (Isaiah 43:11), yet the New Testament calls Jesus Savior (Titus 2:13-14).
Jesus' divine names	Divine names like Yahweh and Elohim are ascribed to Jesus (Isaiah 40:3).
Jesus' divine attributes	Jesus is eternal (Isaiah 9:6), omnipresent (Matthew 28:20; Ephesians 1:22-23), and immutable (Hebrews 13:8).
Jesus' divine activities	Just as Yahweh gives and preserves life in Old Testament times, so Jesus does in New Testament times (John 5:21).
Jesus' divine characteristics	As Yahweh's voice is said to be "like the roar of rushing waters" (Ezekiel 43:2), so the same is true of the glorified Jesus (Revelation 1:15).
Worship	Jesus was worshipped on many occasions (Matthew 2:11; 8:2; 9:18; 15:25). Only God can be worshipped (Exodus 34:14).

A Comparison of Yahweh and Jesus

Description	Used of Yahweh	Used of Jesus
Yahweh	Exodus 3:14	John 8:24,58
God	Genesis 1:1	John 1:1,14
Alpha and Omega	Isaiah 41:4; 48:12	Revelation 1:8,17-18; 22:12-16
Lord	Isaiah 45:23-25	Philippians 2:10-11
Savior	Isaiah 43:3,11	Titus 2:13-14
Redeemer	Psalm 130:7-8	Ephesians 1:7
Shepherd	Psalm 23:1	John 10:11
Creator	Genesis 1:1	John 1:2-3,10
Omnipresent	Psalm 139:7-12	Matthew 18:20; 28:20
Omniscient	Jeremiah 17:9-10	John 2:25; 16:30
Omnipotent	Isaiah 40:10-31	Matthew 28:18
Preexistent	Genesis 1:1	John 1:15,30; 17:5
Eternal	Psalm 102:26-27	Isaiah 9:6
Immutable	Malachi 3:6	Hebrews 13:8
Speaks with divine authority	"This is what the LORD says" is used 170 of times in the Old Testament.	"Truly I tell you" (Matthew 23:36) is used 79 times in the Gospels.

Names and Titles of Jesus Christ

Name	Scripture	Meaning
Almighty	Revelation 1:8	Jesus is all-powerful.
Bridegroom	John 3:29	Jesus intimately cares for us.
Cornerstone	1 Peter 2:6	Jesus is the rock of Christianity and the rock of our lives.
Immanuel	Matthew 1:23	Jesus is "God with us."
Everlasting Father	Isaiah 9:6	Jesus is eternal.
Firstborn	Colossians 1:15	Jesus is preeminent over the creation.
Head of the church	Ephesians 5:23	Jesus leads the church.
King of kings	Revelation 17:14	Jesus is sovereign over all the universe.
Lamb of God	John 1:29,36	Jesus is our substitutionary sacrifice.
Light of the world	John 8:12	Jesus is the spiritual light of all humankind.

Name	Scripture	Meaning
Messiah	John 1:41	Jesus is the Christ (the anointed one).
Prince of peace	Isaiah 9:6	Jesus is our peace.
Prophet	Deuteronomy 18:15-22; Luke 7:16	Jesus reveals God's word.
Redeemer	Job 19:25	Jesus redeems us from sin.
Savior	John 4:42	Jesus saves us from sin.
Shepherd	1 Peter 2:25	Jesus walks with us and watches over us.
Son of God	Luke 1:35	Jesus is God's Son by nature (divine).
True vine	John 15:1	Jesus is our source of spiritual nourishment.
Wonderful Counselor	Isaiah 9:6	Jesus is our defense attorney.
Word	John 1:1	Jesus is God's ultimate revelation.

Christ's Humanity (the Incarnation)

Jesus was fully divine but also fully human in the incarnation (John 1:14; Colossians 2:9).

Jesus had human parents.	Matthew 1:18-19
Jesus experienced a human birth.	Matthew 1:23; Luke 2:6-7
Jesus experienced normal human growth.	Luke 2:40-52
Jesus had human ethnicity—He was Jewish.	John 4:9; Galatians 4:4; Hebrews 7:14
Jesus had human relatives.	Mark 6:3; John 7:5
Jesus experienced normal human emotions.	John 11:35; Hebrews 5:7
Jesus experienced normal human hunger and thirst.	Luke 4:2; John 4:1-7; 19:28
Jesus experienced normal human fatigue.	Mark 6:31; John 4:6
Jesus experienced human pain.	Matthew 26:46; Mark 15:25-34; John 19:28
Jesus experienced human death.	Matthew 27:50; Mark 15:37; Luke 23:46; John 19:30; 1 Corinthians 15:3

Two Natures in the Incarnate Christ

Before the incarnation	Jesus was one person with one nature (a divine nature).
After the incarnation	Jesus was still one person but now had two natures—divine and human.
Two natures in one person	Though Jesus in the incarnation had a human and divine nature, He was one person. He consistently used singular pronouns (I, me, and mine) in reference to Himself.
Seemingly contradictory qualities	Christ in the incarnation had what seem to be contradictory qualities. He was finite and yet infinite, weak and yet omnipotent, increasing in knowledge and yet omniscient.
The union lasts forever	When Christ became a man in the incarnation, He did not enter into a temporary union of the human and divine in one person. Christ's human nature continues forever (see Matthew 26:64; Acts 1:11).

Jesus the Divine Son of God

Meaning of "Son of"	Ancient Semitics used the phrase "Son of" to indicate equality of being.
Jewish understanding	When Jesus claimed to be the Son of God, His Jewish contemporaries understood that He was making an unqualified claim to be God. "The Jews were seeking all the more to kill him, because...he was even calling God his own Father, making himself equal with God" (John 5:18 NASB; see also 19:7).
Eternal sonship	God created the universe through His Son (Hebrews 1:2). Christ was the Son of God prior to the creation. Christ existed as the Son "before all things" (Colossians 1:17). Jesus asserted His eternal preexistence before Abraham (John 8:54-58).

Jesus Was Sinless

He was innocent.	Judas admitted that Jesus was innocent when he betrayed Him (Matthew 27:4).
He had no falsehood.	There is nothing false about Jesus (John 7:18). He always did what pleased the Father (John 8:29).
He had no sin.	Jesus challenged Jewish leaders, "Can any of you prove me guilty of sin?" (John 8:46). None ever could. The apostle Paul referred to Jesus as "him who had no sin" (2 Corinthians 5:21). "He did not sin" (Hebrews 4:15).
He loved righteousness.	Jesus is one who "loved righteousness and hated wickedness" (Hebrews 1:9).
He was blameless.	Jesus was holy, blameless, and pure (Hebrews 7:26).
He had no deceit.	Jesus "committed no sin, and no deceit was found in his mouth" (1 Peter 2:22). "In him is no sin" (1 John 3:5).

The Incarnate Christ Could Not Have Sinned

He is immutable.	In His divine nature, Jesus does not change.
He is omniscient.	In His divine nature, Jesus knows all the consequences of sin.
He is omnipotent.	In His divine nature, Jesus has more than enough power to resist sin.
He is not susceptible.	Temptability does not imply susceptibility. Christ was genuinely tempted, but He was not susceptible to sin.
He overcame temptation.	Hebrews 4 tells us that Jesus was tempted yet was without sin.
He had no sin nature.	Unlike all other human beings, Christ had no sin nature and was perfectly holy from birth (Luke 1:35).
Illustration	If a canoe attacked a US battleship, the attack would be genuine but would stand no chance of success. Christ's temptations were genuine but stood no chance of luring Him to sin.

Jesus Was a Miracle Worker

Jesus' signs	John referred to the miracles of Jesus as signs (John 2:11; 4:54; 6:14; 9:16). Jesus performed these signs to signify His true identity and glory as the divine Messiah (Isaiah 35:5-6).
An adequate witness	John tells us that Jesus consistently performed His signs in the presence of His disciples (John 20:30). Jesus' signs are thoroughly attested.
Many miracles	The Gospels record 35 of Christ's miracles. These are only a selection from among many that He did (see Matthew 4:23-24; 11:4-5; John 20:30; 21:25).
The purpose of miracles	Jesus' miracles or signs were recorded in Scripture so that we may believe that Jesus is the Christ, the Son of God (John 20:31).

The Offices of Christ

Jesus, the divine Messiah, fulfilled the three primary offices of prophet, priest, and king.

Prophet	As a prophet, Jesus gave major discourses, including the Sermon on the Mount (Matthew 5–7), the Olivet Discourse (Matthew 24–25), and the Upper Room Discourse (John 14–16). He also spoke as a prophet on many occasions on the subject of the kingdom of God (see Luke 4:43).
Priest	As our divine high priest, Jesus represents God the Father to us and represents us to God the Father. He is our mediator (1 Timothy 2:5). Jesus also performed the ultimate sacrifice—He shed His own blood on our behalf (Hebrews 7:27)—and continues to pray on our behalf (verse 25).

King	Genesis 49:10 prophesied that the Messiah would reign as a King. The Davidic covenant promised that the Messiah would have an eternal throne (2 Samuel 7:16). In Psalm 2:6, the Father announces the installation of His Son as King. Psalm 110 affirms that the Messiah will reign. Daniel 7:13-14 tells us that the Messiah-King will have an everlasting dominion. An angel appeared to Mary with this message: "He will reign over Jacob's descendants forever; his kingdom will never end" (Luke 1:33). When Jesus comes again, He will come as the King of kings and Lord of lords (Revelation 19:16; see also 17:14).
Summary	As a prophet, Jesus reveals. As a high priest, Jesus redeems and represents. As a King, Jesus reigns.

Jesus Atoned for Sin

He was born to die.	Jesus affirmed that the crucifixion was the very reason He came into the world (John 12:27).
He was a sacrificial offering.	Jesus knew His death was a sacrificial offering for the sins of humanity. He said His blood would be "poured out for many for the forgiveness of sins" (Matthew 26:26-28).
We have no hope without Him.	Jesus took His sacrificial mission with utmost seriousness, for He knew that without Him, humanity would certainly perish (Matthew 16:25; John 3:16) and spend eternity apart from God in a place of great suffering (Matthew 10:28; 11:23; 23:33; 25:41; Luke 16:22-28).
Jesus' mission	Jesus described His mission this way: "The Son of Man did not come to be served, but to serve, and to give his life a ransom for many" (Matthew 20:28).

Major Events of Passion Week

Day	Event	Scripture
Sunday a.m.	Triumphal entry	Matthew 21:1-17
Monday a.m.	Cursing of fig tree	Mark 11:12-14
Tuesday a.m.	Jesus' authority is challenged	Matthew 21:23–23:39
Tuesday p.m.	Olivet Discourse	Matthew 24–25
Wednesday a.m.	Jesus' betrayal is planned	Matthew 26:1-5
Thursday p.m.	The Last Supper	John 13
Thursday p.m.	Upper Room Discourse	John 13–17
Friday a.m.	Betrayal and arrest	Matthew 26:47-56
Friday a.m.	Trials before the Sanhedrin, Pilate, and Herod	Matthew 26:57–27:26; Luke 23:6-12
Friday p.m.	Crucifixion and burial	Matthew 27:27-56
Sunday a.m.	Resurrection and subsequent appearances	Matthew 28; Luke 24:13-49; John 20:1-18

Key Evidences for the Resurrection

Jesus appeared first to Mary.	Jesus first attested to His resurrection by appearing to Mary Magdalene (John 20:1). This indicates the authenticity and reliability of the resurrection account. No one in a first-century Jewish culture would have invented the account this way. A woman's testimony carried no weight in biblical times.
Jesus appeared to the disciples.	The risen Christ appeared to the disciples and said to them, "Peace be with you" (John 20:19)—a common Hebrew greeting (see 1 Samuel 25:6). Jesus immediately showed them His hands and His side to prove it was really Him (John 20:20).
The disciples became fearless.	The disciples came away from the crucifixion frightened and full of doubt. But overnight, they were transformed into bulwarks of courage, fearless defenders of the faith. Only the resurrection can explain this.

Jesus provided many convincing proofs.	"He presented himself to them and gave many convincing proofs that he was alive. He appeared to them over a period of forty days and spoke about the kingdom of God" (Acts 1:3). Jesus appeared to too many people on too many occasions over too long a time for the resurrection to be dismissed.
Jesus appeared to 500 at a time.	The resurrected Jesus "appeared to more than five hundred of the brothers and sisters at the same time" (1 Corinthians 15:6). None of these 500 stepped forward to dispute the resurrection claim.
Thousands of Jews were converted.	Thousands of Jews left Judaism and its rituals and requirements—which had been ingrained in them from childhood—to follow Jesus. Only the resurrection of Jesus can explain why they left the religion of their families to follow the carpenter from Nazareth.

Jesus Was Physically Resurrected

Jesus' physical resurrected body	The resurrected Christ said, "Look at my hands and my feet. It is I myself! Touch me and see; a ghost does not have flesh and bones, as you see I have" (Luke 24:39). He indicates that He is not a spirit, that His resurrection body has flesh and bones, and that His hands and feet are proof of His physical resurrection.
Jesus' promise	Jesus promised the Jews, "Destroy this temple, and I will raise it again in three days." He was referring to His physical body (John 2:19-21).
Jesus ate physical food	On several occasions, the resurrected Christ ate food to prove He had a real physical body (Luke 24:30,42-43; John 21:12-13).
Touched and handled	Various people touched and handled the physical body of the resurrected Christ (Matthew 28:9; Luke 24:39; John 20:17,27; 1 John 1:1).
Sown and raised	The body "sown" in death is the same body that is raised in life (1 Corinthians 15:35-44).

5

The Holy Spirit

The Holy Spirit Is God

Evidence	Scripture
Treated as God	Acts 5:3-4 equates lying to the Holy Spirit and lying to God.
Called Lord	In 2 Corinthians 3:17-18 the Holy Spirit is called Lord.
Identified with Yahweh	The Holy Spirit is often identified with Yahweh (Acts 7:51; 28:25-27; 1 Corinthians 2:12-13; Hebrews 3:7-9; 2 Peter 1:21).
Divine	The Holy Spirit is divine (Matthew 12:32; Mark 3:29; 1 Corinthians 3:16; 6:19; Ephesians 2:22).
The Spirit of God	The Holy Spirit is the "Spirit of God," which indicates His full deity (Genesis 1:2; Exodus 31:3; Romans 8:9,14; 1 Corinthians 2:11,14).
Attributes of deity	The Holy Spirit is omnipresent (Psalm 139:7), omniscient (1 Corinthians 2:10), omnipotent (Romans 15:19), holy (John 16:7-14), and eternal (Hebrews 9:14).

The Holy Spirit Is a Person

He has personal attributes.	The three primary attributes of personality are intellect, emotions, and will. The Holy Spirit has all three.
He has a mind.	Romans 8:27 tells us that just as the Holy Spirit knows the things of God, so the Father knows "what the mind of the Spirit is."
He has emotions.	Ephesians 4:30 admonishes, "Do not grieve the Holy Spirit of God." Grief is an emotion.
He has a will.	We are told in 1 Corinthians 12:11 that the Holy Spirit distributes spiritual gifts "to each one individually just as He wills."
He engages in works only a person can do.	The Holy Spirit teaches believers (John 14:26), testifies (John 15:26), commissions people to service (Acts 13:4), issues commands to believers (Acts 8:29), and intercedes for believers (Romans 8:26).

Names and Titles of the Holy Spirit

Name/Title	Scripture	Meaning
Helper	John 14:16,26	He helps and comforts believers.
Eternal Spirit	Hebrews 9:14	He is eternal God.
Holy Spirit	Luke 11:13	He is holy and completely pure.
Lord	2 Corinthians 3:16-17	He is the sovereign Lord.
Power of the Most High	Luke 1:35	His power is immeasurable.
Spirit of glory	1 Peter 4:14	He glorifies Jesus.
Spirit of God	1 Corinthians 2:11	He is God.
Spirit of the LORD	Isaiah 11:2; 61:1	He is Yahweh and is sovereign.
Spirit of truth	John 14:17; 15:26	He is truth by nature and communicates truth.
Spirit of the living God	2 Corinthians 3:3	He is the Spirit of the God of life.
Spirit of prophecy	Revelation 19:10	He inspires prophecy.

Spiritual Gifts

Gift	Function	Scripture
Prophecy	Speaking truth from God—fore-telling the future or proclaiming the truth	Romans 12:6; 1 Corinthians 14:29-32
Service, helping	Helping others in the body of Christ	Romans 12:7
Teaching	Communicating scriptural truth	Romans 12:7
Encouraging	Exhorting the body of Christ	Romans 12:8
Giving	Meeting the physical needs of church members	Romans 12:8
Leadership	Administering the work of ministry	Romans 12:8
Showing mercy	Giving under-served help to others	Romans 12:8
Apostleship	Witnessing the resurrected Christ and speaking authoritatively for God	1 Corinthians 12:28; Ephesians 4:11

Gift	Function	Scripture
Evangelism	Sharing the gospel	Ephesians 4:11
Pastor/teacher	Shepherding and teaching God's people	Romans 12:7; Ephesians 4:11
Message of wisdom	Perceiving and sharing God's truth	1 Corinthians 12:8
Message of knowledge	Perceiving and sharing God's wisdom	1 Corinthians 12:8
Faith	Trusting God in a special way	1 Corinthians 12:9
Healing	Curing disease with God's power	1 Corinthians 12:9
Miracles	Performing works of power from God	1 Corinthians 12:10
Discernment	Distinguishing a spirit speaking through a person	1 Corinthians 12:10
Tongues	Speaking in an unknown language	1 Corinthians 12:10
Interpretation	Helping others understand a message in another tongue	1 Corinthians 12:10

Is the Gift of Tongues for Today?

Yes	No
Speaking in tongues is an evidence of the baptism of the Holy Spirit (Acts 2:4).	Not all the Corinthians spoke in tongues (1 Corinthians 14:5), but all were baptized (12:13).
Speaking in tongues should be normative among Christians today.	The Holy Spirit bestows spiritual gifts (1 Corinthians 12:11). Not every Christian has every gift.
Speaking in tongues is the test of being filled with the Holy Spirit.	The fruit of the Holy Spirit (Galatians 5:22-23) does not include speaking in tongues. Therefore, Christlikeness does not require this gift.
Speaking in tongues is a biblical doctrine.	Most New Testament writers are silent on tongues. Only three books (Acts, 1 Corinthians, and Mark) mention it.
There is no indication in the New Testament that any of the spiritual gifts have passed away.	First Corinthians 13:8 indicates that tongues would eventually cease of their own accord.
Speaking in tongues is an inheritance of the sons of God.	Other gifts are more important than tongues, and these are to be sought (1 Corinthians 12:28,31).

Yes	No
The New Testament books are written for believers of all time periods. Tongues are found throughout the New Testament, so there is no reason they shouldn't be experienced today.	Sign gifts (such as speaking in tongues) miraculously confirmed the message revealed to the apostles (Acts 2:22; 3:3-11; 5:15-16; 9:36-42). Once that message was completed, there was no further need for confirmation (see Hebrews 2:3-4).
Jesus is the same yesterday, today, and forever (Hebrews 13:8). He doesn't change, so His gift of tongues to believers has not changed either.	Though Jesus does not change, His plan and purpose for people in different times do change. It may not be His purpose for all generations to have the gift of speaking in tongues.

The Work of the Holy Spirit in Salvation

Work	Description	Scripture
Regeneration	The Spirit gives new life.	John 3:3-8; Titus 3:5
Indwelling	The Spirit abides in believers.	John 14:17; Romans 8:9
Baptizing	Believers are baptized in the Holy Spirit by Christ.	Mark 1:8; Luke 3:16; 1 Corinthians 12:13
Sealing	Believers are sealed with the Spirit.	Ephesians 1:13; 4:30
Filling	Believers are controlled by the Holy Spirit.	Ephesians 5:18
Guiding	Believers are led by the Spirit.	Galatians 5:16,25
Empowering	Believers are empowered by the Holy Spirit to live victoriously.	Romans 8:13; Galatians 5:17-18,22-23
Teaching	The Spirit leads believers into truth.	John 14:26; 16:13
Interceding	The Holy Spirit prays for believers.	Romans 8:26

6

Humanity

The Equality of the Races

God created everyone.

The apostle Paul affirmed, "From one man he made all the nations, that they should inhabit the whole earth; and he marked out their appointed times in history and the boundaries of their lands" (Acts 17:26).

People are completely equal.

All people are equal in terms of...

- their creation (Genesis 1:27-28)
- their sin problem (Romans 3:23)
- their going astray in life as a result of sin (Isaiah 53:6)
- God's love for each of them (John 3:16)
- God's provision of salvation for each of them (Matthew 28:19)

The redeemed

Revelation 5:9 tells us that God's redeemed will be from "every tribe and language and people and nation."

Conclusion

There is no place for racial discrimination, for all human beings are equal in God's sight.

Six Arguments Against Evolution

Argument	Significance
Scientists largely agree that the universe had a beginning.	The fact that there was a beginning implies the existence of a Beginner—a Creator. Hebrews 3:4 says, "Every house is built by someone, but God is the builder of everything."
Observing the universe reveals that a Designer was involved.	Everything is perfect for life on earth—so fine-tuned that it gives every evidence of coming from the hands of an intelligent Designer (God). For example, the earth's size, composition, distance from the sun, and rotational period are all just right for life.
The fossil records provide evidence against evolution.	If evolution were true, one would expect to see in the fossil records progressively complex evolutionary forms, indicating evolutionary transitions that took place. No transitional links have been discovered in the fossil records.

Argument	Significance
Evolution assumes a long series of positive and upward mutations.	Mutations are almost always not beneficial, but rather are harmful to living beings. Deformities typically lessen the survival potential of an animal rather than strengthening it.
The first and second laws of thermodynamics militate against evolution.	The first law says that matter and energy are neither created nor destroyed; they just change forms. The second law says that in an isolated system (such as our universe), the natural course of things is to degenerate. Our universe is running down, not evolving upward.
Evolutionists often make false claims.	Mutations within species is a proven scientific fact. (This is called "microevolution.") An incredible leap of logic is required to say that mutations within species proves mutations into entirely new species ("macroevolution").

Humans Are Not Divine

Contrary to what some cults teach, humans are not divine.

God's Attributes	Human Attributes
God knows everything (Psalm 147:5; Romans 11:33).	Human knowledge is limited (Job 38:4).
God can do anything (Revelation 19:6).	People are weak (Hebrews 4:15).
God is everywhere (Psalm 139:7-12).	Humans are confined to a single space at a time (John 1:50).
God is holy (1 John 1:5).	People's best efforts are as filthy garments before God (Isaiah 64:6).
God is eternal (Psalm 90:2).	Humans are created at a point in time (Genesis 1:1,21,27).
God is truth (John 14:6).	The human heart is deceitful (Jeremiah 17:9).
God is just (Acts 17:31).	Humans are lawless (Romans 3:23; 1 John 3:4).
God is love (Ephesians 2:4-5).	Humans are plagued with numerous vices, such as jealousy and strife (1 Corinthians 3:3).

Humans Don't Become Angels at Death

Colossians 1:16	Christ created the angels as angels.
Psalm 8:5	Human beings were made lower than the angels but will be higher than the angels in in heaven.
Hebrews 12:22-23	In heaven, the "myriads of angels" are distinct from the "spirits of righteous men made perfect."
1 Corinthians 6:3	Believers will someday judge angels.
1 Corinthians 13:1	Humans and angels use different languages.
Luke 16:22	Angels escort the spirits of dead (human) believers into heaven.
1 Thessalonians 4:14-17; 1 John 3:2	Dead believers will be resurrected as humans, just as Jesus was, not as angels.

Conclusion
The Bible consistently distinguishes human beings from angels.

7

Sin and Salvation

	Jesus on Human Sin
Lost sinners	• Human beings are by nature evil (Matthew 12:34; Luke 11:13).
	• They are capable of great wickedness (Mark 7:20-23; Luke 11:42-52).
	• They are utterly lost (Luke 19:10).
	• They are sinners (Luke 15:10) in need of repentance before a holy God (Mark 1:15).
Metaphors for sin	• blindness (Matthew 23:16-26)
	• sickness (Matthew 9:12)
	• slavery (John 8:34)
	• darkness (John 3:19-21; 8:12; 12:35-46)
A universal problem	Jesus taught that this is a universal condition and that all people are guilty before God (see Luke 7:37-48).
Internal and external	Jesus taught that not only external acts but also inner thoughts render a person guilty of sin (Matthew 5:28).

Conclusion
Humankind desperately needs salvation.

God's Purpose for the Law

It cannot save.	God did not give us the law as a means of attaining salvation. Romans 3:20 emphasizes that "no one will be declared righteous in God's sight by the works of the law."
It shows us what sin is.	God gave us the law to show us what sin is. The law revealed God's holy standards of conduct. The law also shows us the consequences if we do not measure up to those high standards.
It provokes sin.	The law also provokes sin all the more in human beings. It was given "so that the trespass might increase" (Romans 5:20). God wants us to become so overwhelmed with the sin problem that we cannot deny its reality and our need for a Savior.
It is like a tutor.	The law is like a tutor or guardian that leads us to Christ (Galatians 3:24-25). The law does this by showing us our sin and then pointing to the marvelous grace of Christ.
It is no longer binding.	Once we have come to Christ—trusting in Him as our Savior—the law has done its job and no longer holds sway over us (Romans 10:4).

Salvation Terms

Born again	Literally means "born from above." It refers to God's gift of eternal life to those who believe in Christ (Titus 3:5).
Justified	God acquits and declares righteous all those who believe in Jesus. "Since we have been justified through faith, we have peace with God through our Lord Jesus Christ" (Romans 5:1).
Reconciled	Those who believe in Jesus are no longer estranged from God. "God was reconciling the world to himself in Christ, not counting people's sins against them. And he has committed to us the message of reconciliation" (2 Corinthians 5:19).
Forgiven	God said, "Their sins and lawless acts I will remember no more" (Hebrews 10:17).
Adopted	Believers are adopted into God's family (Romans 8:14). They now await their family inheritance (Colossians 3:24).

Distinctive Roles of the Father, Son, and Holy Spirit

The Father's role	The Father devised the plan of salvation (Ephesians 1:4-5). He sovereignly decreed it in eternity past (Romans 8:29-30). The plan included the means of salvation (Jesus' death on the cross), the objective (the forgiveness of sins), and the persons to benefit (believers).
Jesus' role	Jesus was the mediator between the Father and humankind (1 Timothy 2:5). He died on the cross as a sacrifice for the sins of humanity (John 3:16) and purchased the church with His precious blood (Revelation 5:9).
The Holy Spirit's role	The Holy Spirit regenerates believers—He gives them new, spiritual life (Titus 3:5). He seals believers for the day of redemption (Ephesians 4:30) and enables believers to live victoriously (Galatians 5:22-23).

The Justification of Believers

Definition

Justification is an instantaneous event in which God judicially declares the believing sinner to be not guilty and absolutely righteous (Romans 3:25-30; Galatians 4:21–5:12).

By faith	We become justified the moment we trust in Christ (Romans 3:28).
External to man	This legal declaration is something external to man. It does not hinge on man's personal level of righteousness, but rather hinges solely on God's declaration.
Once and for all	Justification is a once-and-for-all judicial pronouncement. Even while the person is yet a sinner and is experientially not righteous, he is nevertheless righteous in God's sight because of forensic justification. This takes place at conversion.

Salvation by Grace Through Faith

Grace

Salvation is "by grace through faith" (Ephesians 2:8-9).
"Grace" means "unmerited favor." "Unmerited" means it can't
be earned. Grace refers to the undeserved, unearned favor of
God (Romans 5:1-11).

A Gift

"The gift of God is eternal life in Christ Jesus our Lord"
(Romans 6:23; see also Revelation 21:6). Titus 3:5 tells us that
God "saved us, not because of righteous things we had done,
but because of his mercy."

Faith

Salvation is a free gift of grace that comes as a result of believing in the Savior, Jesus Christ. "Everyone who believes in him
may have eternal life in him" (John 3:15). "Very truly I tell
you, whoever hears my word and believes him who sent me
has eternal life and will not be judged, but has crossed over
from death to life" (John 5:24). "Very truly, I tell you, the one
who believes has eternal life" (John 6:47).

Two Views of Election

Election is the sovereign act of God whereby He chose certain individuals to salvation before the foundation of the world. There are two primary views.

The Foreknowledge View	The Sovereignty View
God's election is based on His foreknowledge of who will respond favorably to the gospel.	God's election is based on His sovereign choice alone.
God's salvation has appeared to all human beings, not merely the elect (Titus 2:11).	Certain human beings have been given to Christ (John 6:37; 17:2), and the Father draws them to Christ (John 6:44).
Christ died for all (1 Timothy 2:6; 4:10; Hebrews 2:9; 2 Peter 2:1; 1 John 2:2).	Christ died for the church (Acts 20:28) and for His sheep (John 10:11).
Everyone is called to turn to God (Isaiah 31:6), repent (Matthew 3:2), and believe (John 6:29).	All who are appointed to eternal life believe (Acts 13:48).

The Five Points of Calvinism

Doctrine	Explanation
Total depravity	Humans are not completely devoid of good impulses. But all people are engulfed in sin to such a degree that they can do nothing to earn merit before God (Romans 3:10-12; 6:20).
Unconditional election	God's choice of certain persons to salvation does not depend on any foreseen virtue on their part, but rather is based entirely on His sovereignty (Romans 9:11,15,21; Ephesians 1:4-8).
Limited atonement	Christ's atoning death was only for the elect and not for all people (Matthew 25:32-33; 26:28; John 10:11,15; 17:9).
Irresistible grace	Those whom God has chosen for eternal life will, as a result of God's irresistible grace, come to faith and thus come to salvation (John 1:12-13; 6:28-29).
Perseverance of the saints	Those who are genuine believers will endure in the faith to the end (John 6:47; 10:27-28; Romans 8:1; Philippians 1:6).

Arminianism

Doctrine	Explanation
Election based on foreknowledge	God elected those whom He foreknew would, of their own free wills, believe in Christ and persevere in the faith (1 Peter 1:1-2).
Unlimited atonement	Christ provided redemption for all humankind, making all humans savable (1 John 2:2). Christ's atonement becomes effective only in those who believe (Acts 16:31).
Natural inability	Humans cannot save themselves (Romans 3:10-11). The Holy Spirit must effect the new birth.
Prevenient grace	Prevenient grace from the Holy Spirit enables one to respond to the gospel (Acts 16:14).
Conditional perseverance	Believers have been empowered to live victoriously. They are also capable of turning from grace and losing salvation (2 Timothy 4:2-4; Hebrews 12:25; 2 Peter 2:21).

Limited Atonement

Limited atonement is the view that Christ died not for all people, but only for the elect.

"She will give birth to a Son, and you are to give him the name Jesus, because he will save *his people* from their sins" (Matthew 1:21).

"The Son of Man did not come to be served, but to serve, and to give his life as a ransom *for many*" (Matthew 20:28).

"I lay down my life *for the sheep*" (John 10:15).

"Keep watch over yourselves and all the flock of which the Holy Spirit has made you overseers. Be shepherds of *the church of God*, which he bought with his own blood" (Acts 20:28).

"Husbands, love your wives, just as Christ loved *the church* and gave himself up *for her*" (Ephesians 5:25).

"Christ was offered once to take away the sins *of many*" (Hebrews 9:28).

"Greater love has no one than this: to lay down one's life *for one's friends*" (John 15:13).

Unlimited Atonement

Unlimited atonement is the view that Christ's redemptive death was for all persons.

"For the Son of Man came to seek and to save *the lost*" (Luke 19:10).

"Look, the Lamb of God, who takes away the sin *of the world*" (John 1:29).

"We have put our hope in the living God, who is the Savior *of all people*, and especially of those who believe" (1 Timothy 4:10).

"At just the right time…Christ died *for the ungodly*" (Romans 5:6).

"Consequently, just as one trespass resulted in condemnation for *all people*, so also one righteous act resulted in justification and life for *all people*" (Romans 5:18).

"He is the atoning sacrifice for our sins, and *not only for ours only but also for the sins of the whole world*" (1 John 2:2).

"*We all*, like sheep, have gone astray…and the LORD has laid on him the iniquity *of us all*" (Isaiah 53:6).

Universalism

Universalist Arguments	Biblical Answers
A sovereign God would never devise a plan in which some end up in hell for all eternity.	God has given humans free will. Those who freely reject God are eternally quarantined.
It is not right to condemn a person to hell based on decisions made during a short earthly life.	One's life on earth is plenty of time to choose for or against God.
God desires that all people be saved (1 Timothy 2:3-4; 2 Peter 3:9), so all will be saved.	God desires all to be saved, but not all humans accept His offer of salvation (John 5:40).
Christ died for all, so all will be saved (see Romans 5:18; 1 Corinthians 15:22).	Christ died for all, but the benefits of that death are applied only to those who trust in Christ (Acts 16:31).
Philippians 2:10-11 assures us that someday all people will acknowledge that Jesus is Lord.	Not all people will necessarily acknowledge Christ as Savior. Even those in hell acknowledge Christ's lordship.

Is Healing Included in the Atonement?

Yes	No
Isaiah 53:5 says we are healed through Christ's wounds.	Isaiah 53:5 refers to spiritual healing from sin, not physical healing.
Going to a doctor shows a lack of faith.	Jesus Himself said, "It is not the healthy who need a doctor, but the sick" (Matthew 9:12).
It is not God's will for anyone to be sick.	Sometimes God has a purpose in allowing us to go through times of suffering (1 Peter 4:15-19).
People in biblical times were healed.	God allowed Epaphroditus (Philippians 2:25-27), Trophimus (2 Timothy 4:20), Timothy (1 Timothy 5:23), Job (Job 1–2), and Paul (2 Corinthians 12:9) to suffer periods of sickness.
Physical healing is guaranteed in the atonement.	*Ultimate* physical healing (in the resurrection body) is guaranteed in the atonement.

8

The Church

Local Churches and the Universal Church

Local Churches	The Universal Church
Include both saved and lost people	Includes only saved people
Include only living people	Includes living and dead believers in Christ, from Pentecost to the rapture
Are scattered throughout the world	Is one worldwide church
Are categorized into many different denominations	Is not denominational. All who trust in Christ for salvation are members regardless of their denominational affiliation.
Include only part of the body of Christ (only living believers)	Includes all of the body of Christ (both dead and living members)
Operate under various forms of church government, such as congregational, presbyterian, and episcopal	Christ alone is the head of the universal church.

The Day of Worship

Saturday	Sunday
God made the Sabbath at creation for all people (Genesis 2:2-3).	New Testament believers are not under the Old Testament law (Romans 6:14).
Christ observed the Sabbath (Mark 1:21) and is the Lord of the Sabbath (Mark 2:28).	Jesus rose from the dead and appeared to some of His followers on a Sunday (Matthew 28:1).
The apostle Paul preached on the Sabbath (Acts 17:2).	Jesus made continuing resurrection appearances on Sundays (John 20:26). John had his apocalyptic vision on a Sunday (Revelation 1:10).
Gentiles worshipped on the Sabbath (Acts 13:42-44).	The descent of the Holy Spirit was on a Sunday (Acts 2:1).
Matthew, Mark, and Luke, writing after the resurrection, spoke of the Sabbath as an existing institution (Matthew 24:20; Mark 16:1; Luke 23:56).	The early church was given the pattern of Sunday worship and continued to follow it regularly (Acts 20:7; 1 Corinthians 16:2).

Are Traditional Hymns Better than Contemporary Music?

Better lyrics	Hymn texts are generally richer, more poetic, and more doctrinal than contemporary song lyrics.
Mature authors	Many hymns were written by spiritual giants of the past, including Martin Luther and Charles Wesley.
Appeal to older church members	Many churchgoers are accustomed to hymns, so churches that introduce contemporary music risk losing some faithful attenders.
Not overly loud	The volume of contemporary music and full bands may detract from the worship.
Not performance oriented	Contemporary music can become showy and performance oriented. This detracts from true worship.

Is Contemporary Music Better than Traditional Hymns?

More accessible for unchurched people	Most unchurched people have never sung hymns and can more easily relate to contemporary worship music.
Luther's example	Martin Luther put Christian words to some of the popular bar songs of his day.
Contemporary hymns	Some of today's contemporary artists are writing hymns, so there should be no objection to using them in worship.
Familiarity	Many churchgoers listen to Christian radio and are already familiar with contemporary worship songs.
Designed for worship	Some of today's praise choruses have been specifically designed to be conducive to worship.

The Mode of Baptism

Sprinkling or Pouring	Immersion
A secondary meaning of the Greek word *baptizo* is "to bring under the influence of." This fits the idea of sprinkling or pouring water on the one being baptized.	The primary meaning of the Greek word *baptizo* is "to immerse." Prepositions used in conjunction with *baptizo* (such as "into" and "out of" the water) picture immersion.
Baptism by sprinkling or pouring best pictures the coming of the Holy Spirit upon a person.	Baptism by immersion best pictures death to the old life and resurrection to the new life in Jesus Christ (Romans 6:1-4).
There was probably not enough water to baptize so many people in the Jerusalem area in New Testament times (Acts 2:41; 8:38).	Archaeologists have now uncovered ancient pools all over the Jerusalem area. There was more than enough water and pools to baptize the thousands of first-century converts.

The Baptism of Infants

Yes	No
Baptism is like Old Testament circumcision, which was performed on infants (Colossians 2:11-12).	Baptism is not the New Testament equivalent of circumcision (a sign of the old covenant that involved only males). Baptism follows conversion (Acts 16:29-34).
Households were baptized in the New Testament (Acts 16:15,33; 18:8). These surely included infants.	Household baptisms did not necessarily include infants. Nowhere does Scripture say that infants were included in household baptisms (see Acts 18:8, 1 Corinthians 1:16; 16:15).
Baptism is essential to salvation, including the salvation of little children (Acts 2:38; 22:16; John 3:5).	Every instance of baptism in the New Testament involved a person old enough to exercise personal faith in Christ (see Acts 16:31; see also John 3:18,36; 20:31; Romans 10:9). Neither Jesus nor His disciples baptized an infant.

Views on the Lord's Supper

Roman Catholic	The bread and wine actually change into the body and blood of Jesus at the prayer of the priest. Jesus is literally present. The sacrament imparts grace to the recipient.
Lutheran	Christ is present in, with, and under the bread and wine. There is a real presence of Christ but no change in the elements. God communicates grace through the elements.
Reformed	Christ is spiritually present at the Lord's Supper. It is a means of grace.
Memorial	There is no change in the elements, and they do not communicate grace to the participant. The bread and wine are symbols and reminders of Jesus' death and resurrection, our anticipation of the second coming, and our oneness as the body of Christ.

The Ordination of Women

Yes	No
Women can be ordained under the authority of a (male) senior pastor.	The disciples and apostles were all male, establishing a pattern of male leadership.
Miriam the prophetess, who helped Moses shepherd Israel, illustrates women in leadership (Exodus 15).	Genesis to Revelation provides a pattern of male leadership. Female prophetesses were rare.
If women can prophesy (1 Corinthians 11:5), they can participate in any ministry.	An elder must be faithful to his wife (1 Timothy 3:2). This excludes women.
Many gifted women in New Testament times helped care for the lost and bring them to salvation (Mark 15:41).	Paul said women are not permitted to teach or to have authority over men (1 Timothy 2:11-14).
Priscilla (wife of Aquila) helped train Apollos (Acts 18).	Paul said women are to keep silent in church (1 Corinthians 14:33-36).
Women can have the spiritual gift of teaching (Romans 12:7; Ephesians 4:12).	Women are to exercise this gift in nonpastoral roles, such as teaching other women.

9

Angels and Demons

The Roles of Angels

Messengers	The word "angel" literally means "messenger." Angels serve as God's messengers, bringing revelation, announcements, and warnings to God's people (see Daniel 9:20-23; Matthew 1:18-21).
Guardians	God has assigned angels to watch over believers (2 Kings 6:17; Psalm 91:9-11).
Escorts to heaven	At the moment of death, when the soul separates from the body, angels escort believers' souls to their eternal inheritance (Luke 16:22).
Restrainers	Angels sometimes restrain evil among humans. Angels struck some wicked men with blindness so they could not carry out their evil intentions when they came to Lot's house (Genesis 18:22; 19:1,10-11).
Executors of judgment	Angels sometimes execute God's judgments, as when Herod was executed (Acts 12:22-23).

Characteristics of Angels

Incorporeal and invisible	"Incorporeal" means "lacking material form or substance." Angels are not material, physical beings; they are spiritual beings (Hebrews 1:14).
Localized	Angels have to move from one place to another (as did Gabriel—Daniel 9:21-23).
Not all have wings	Many angels in the Bible are described as having wings (Isaiah 6:1-5; Ezekiel 1:6). Other Bible verses about angels make no mention of wings (see Hebrews 13:2). It is possible that all angels have wings, but this is not a necessary inference.
Can appear as men	Though angels are incorporeal and invisible, they can appear as men (Genesis 18). Their resemblance can be so realistic that the angel is taken to be human (Hebrews 13:2).
Powerful	Psalm 103:20 calls them "mighty ones who do [God's] bidding." Second Thessalonians 1:7 mentions God's "powerful angels."

Holy	The word "holy" means "set apart." God's angels are set apart from sin and set apart to God. Angels are often called God's "holy ones" (Job 5:1; 15:15; Psalm 89:7).
Obedient	God's angels do not do their own bidding. They do only God's bidding (Psalm 103:20).
Great knowledge	Angels are not all-knowing (only God is), but they possess great intelligence. Angels were created as a higher order of creatures than humans (see Psalm 8:5) and innately possess a greater knowledge. They also gain ever-increasing knowledge through long observation of human activities.
Immortal	Angels are not subject to death (Luke 20:36). They do not propagate baby angels (Matthew 22:30), so the number of angels remains constant.

Satan's Titles

The adversary (1 Peter 5:8)	Satan opposes Christians and stands against them in every way he can.
Beelzebub (Matthew 12:24)	This word means "lord of the flies," carrying the idea, "lord of filth." Satan corrupts everything he touches.
The devil (Matthew 4:1)	This word carries the idea of "adversary" and "slanderer."
The evil one (1 John 5:19)	He opposes all that is good.
The father of lies (John 8:44)	Satan was the first and greatest liar and deceiver.
A murderer (John 8:44)	This word literally means "man-killer" (see 1 John 3:12,15).
The god of this age (2 Corinthians 4:4)	Satan is not divine, but he governs this current evil age.
A roaring lion (1 Peter 5:8-9)	He is a strong and destructive predator.
The tempter (Matthew 4:3)	His constant purpose is to incite man to sin.

How Fallen Angels Hurt Believers

They tempt believers to sin.	Ephesians 2:1-3; 1 Thessalonians 3:5
They tempt believers to lie and deceive.	Acts 5:3
They tempt believers to commit sexually immoral acts.	1 Corinthians 7:5
They hinder the work of believers, especially those engaged in ministry.	1 Thessalonians 2:18
They wage war against believers.	Ephesians 6:11-12
They sow weeds among believers, seeking to divide them against each other.	Matthew 13:38-39
They instigate factions among believers so believers don't work together in unity.	James 3:13-16
They hinder answers to believers' prayers.	Daniel 10:12-20
They plant doubt in the minds of believers, weakening their faith.	Genesis 3:1-5
They incite persecutions against believers.	Revelation 2:10

10

Biblical Prophecy

An Overview of the End Times

Event	Description
The rapture	The dead in Christ will be instantly raised from the dead, and living Christians will be instantly translated into their resurrection bodies. Both groups will meet Christ in the air (1 Thessalonians 4:13-17).
The tribulation	During this seven-year period, God will pour out His judgments on the earth (Revelation 4–18). Many believe it will follow the rapture.
The second coming	Following the tribulation period, Christ will come again in glory and majesty as King of kings and Lord of lords (Revelation 19:11-16).
The millennial kingdom	Following the second coming, Christ will set up His thousand-year kingdom of righteousness and peace on earth (Revelation 20:1-3).
The eternal state	Following the millennial kingdom, believers will dwell forever in a new heaven and earth. Unbelievers will forever be consigned to hell (Revelation 20:11–21:27).

Benefits of Studying Prophecy

Fulfilled prophecy demonstrates that the Bible is in fact the Word of God (Isaiah 41:21-29; 42:9; 44:7-8; 46:8-11; 2 Peter 3:4-13).

Prophecy makes up a significant part of Scripture, so studying prophecy makes us informed students of the Word of God (2 Timothy 2:15; 1 Peter 1:10-12; 2 Peter 3:16; Revelation 1:3; 22:18-19).

Prophetic Scripture shows that God is in sovereign control of the world (Daniel 9:27; Acts 4:25-29; Philippians 1:6).

Prophecy promotes evangelism (Acts 3:18-24; Hebrews 9:26-27).

Prophecy motivates Christians to live in purity and righteousness until the Lord comes (Philippians 4:5; 1 Thessalonians 3:13; Titus 2:12-13; James 5:7-9; 1 Peter 1:3-7; 2 Peter 3:11-12; 1 John 3:3; 5:23).

Prophecy provides believers with comfort in the midst of grief and sorrow and helps Christians to maintain an eternal perspective (1 Thessalonians 4:13-18; 1 Peter 1:7-9).

Signs of the Times

These prophetic signs will appear during the future tribulation period.

Earth and sky signs	"There will be great earthquakes, famines and pestilences in various places, and fearful events and great signs from heaven" (Luke 21:11).
Moral signs	"In the last days...people will be lovers of themselves, lovers of money, boastful, proud, abusive, disobedient to their parents, ungrateful, unholy, without love...not lovers of the good, treacherous, rash, conceited, lovers of pleasure rather than lovers of God" (2 Timothy 3:1-4).
Religious signs	"People will not put up with sound doctrine. Instead, to suit their own desires, they will gather around them a great number of teachers to say what their itching ears want to hear" (2 Timothy 4:3-4).
Technological signs	Some signs will be made possible by modern technology. The gospel will be preached to every nation (Matthew 24:14). The antichrist will control a one-world economy (Revelation 13:16-17).

The Case for Pretribulationism

Definition

This is the view that Christ will rapture the church before any part of the tribulation begins.

Old Testament evidence	No Old Testament passage on the tribulation mentions the church (Deuteronomy 4:29-30; Jeremiah 30:4-11; Daniel 8:24-27; 12:1-2).
New Testament evidence	No New Testament passage on the tribulation mentions the church (Matthew 24:15-31; 1 Thessalonians 5:4-9).
Wrath	The church is not appointed to wrath (Romans 5:9; 1 Thessalonians 1:9-10; 5:9).
God protects His people	God typically protects His people before judgment falls (see 2 Peter 2:5-9). Noah and his family are an example. The church will likewise be raptured before the tribulation.
Distinct from second coming	The rapture involves Christ coming *for* His saints in the air prior to the tribulation. At the second coming He will come *with* His saints to the earth (Revelation 19; 20:1-6).
Kept from the hour of trial	In Revelation 3:10, Jesus indicates that believers will be saved "out of" (Greek: *ek*) the actual time (hour) of the tribulation.

The Case for Midtribulationism

Definition

This is the view that Christ will rapture the church in the middle of the tribulation. The church will be delivered from the last half of the seventieth week of Daniel (Daniel 9:24-27), which is much more severe than the first half.

The two witnesses	The two witnesses of Revelation 11, who are caught up to heaven in the middle of the tribulation, are believed to be representative of the church.
Deliverance from God's wrath	The church will be delivered from God's wrath (1 Thessalonians 5:9), which, it is argued, is only in the second half of the tribulation. However, the church will not be delivered from the general tribulation in the first half.
The last trumpet	The rapture occurs at the last trumpet (1 Corinthians 15:52), and the seventh trumpet sounds midway in the tribulation (Revelation 11:15-19), so the rapture must occur midway in the tribulation.

The Case for Posttribulationism

Definition

This is the view that Christ will rapture the church after the tribulation at the second coming of Christ. Believers will be "kept through" the tribulation (Revelation 3:10).

The resurrection of believers	Revelation 20:4-6 indicates that believers will be resurrected at the end of the tribulation. This must mean the rapture happens at that time.
Saints in the tribulation	Saints are mentioned as being on earth during the tribulation (Revelation 13:7).
Taken at the second coming	Matthew 24:40, which is in the general context of the second coming, tells us, "Two men will be in the field; one will be taken and the other left."
Late historical support for pretribulationism	Pretribulationism emerged late in church history, finding its origin in John Nelson Darby (1800–1882). The majority of church history allegedly knew nothing of this view.

Christ and the Antichrist: Comparisons and Contrasts

Christ	Antichrist
Performs miracles, signs, and wonders (Matthew 9:32-33; Mark 6:2)	Performs miracles, signs, and wonders (2 Thessalonians 2:9)
Appears in the millennial temple (Ezekiel 43:6-7)	Sits in the tribulation temple (2 Thessalonians 2:4)
Is God (John 1:1-2; 10:36)	Claims to be God (2 Thessalonians 2:4)
Is the Lion from Judah (Revelation 5:5)	Has a mouth like a lion (Revelation 13:2)
Makes a peace covenant with Israel (Ezekiel 37:26)	Makes a peace covenant with Israel (Daniel 9:27)
Causes men to worship God (Revelation 1:6)	Causes men to worship Satan (Revelation 13:3-4)
Followers sealed on their forehead (Revelation 7:4; 14:1)	Followers sealed on their forehead or right hand (Revelation 13:16-18)
Worthy name (Revelation 19:16)	Blasphemous names (Revelation 13:1)
Married to a virtuous bride (Revelation 19:7-9)	Married to a vile prostitute (Revelation 17:3-5)
Crowned with many crowns (Revelation 19:12)	Crowned with ten crowns (Revelation 13:1)

Christ	Antichrist
Is the King of kings (Revelation 19:16)	Is called "the king" (Daniel 11:36)
Sits on a throne (Revelation 3:21; 12:5; 20:11)	Sits on a throne (Revelation 13:2; 16:10)
Sharp sword from His mouth (Revelation 19:15)	Bow in his hand (Revelation 6:2)
Rides a white horse (Revelation 19:11)	Rides a white horse (Revelation 6:2)
Has an army (Revelation 19:14)	Has an army (Revelation 19:19)
Suffered a violent death (Revelation 5:6; 13:8)	Appears to suffer a violent death (Revelation 13:3)
Resurrected (Matthew 28:6)	Apparently resurrected (Revelation 13:3,14)
Second coming (Revelation 19:11-21)	Second coming (Revelation 17:8)
One-thousand-year worldwide kingdom (Revelation 20:1-6)	Three-and-a-half-year worldwide kingdom (Revelation 13:5-8)
Part of the holy Trinity— Father, Son, and Holy Spirit (2 Corinthians 13:14)	Part of an unholy trinity — Satan, antichrist, and false prophet (Revelation 13)

Millennial Views

Premillennialism

"Pre" means "before," and a millennium is a thousand years. This view holds that the second coming of Christ will occur before His thousand-year kingdom of perfect peace and righteousness (Revelation 20:1-10).

Amillennialism

"A" means "no." There will be no literal thousand-year kingdom of Christ. The thousand-year reign metaphorically refers to Christ's present (spiritual) rule from heaven.

Postmillennialism

"Post" means "after." The second coming of Christ will occur after the thousand years. The thousand years is a metaphor for a long period of time that has already begun. Through the church's influence, the world will be Christianized, and then Christ will return.

The Folly of Predicting Dates

People who predict dates for end-time events have been wrong 100 percent of the time.

Predicting these dates may lead to harmful decisions (such as not saving money).

Christians who succumb to predicting these dates may damage their faith when expectations fail.

If people lose confidence in prophecy, it ceases to motivate them to holiness (Titus 2:12-14).

Predicting dates may damage the faith of new or immature believers when the predictions are shown to be false.

Predicting dates may lead to prophetic agnosticism.

Predicting dates can humiliate the cause of Christ.

Predicting dates might sidetrack Christians from their first priority—living daily for Jesus.

The timing of end-time events is in God's hands (Acts 1:7), and we don't have precise details.

11

The Afterlife

The Judgment of Christians

It is universal. "We will all stand before God's judgment seat" (Romans 14:10).

The extent of one's knowledge of God's will is taken into consideration (Luke 12:48).

Works will be judged. "You will reward everyone according to what they have done" (Psalm 62:12).

Thoughts will be judged. "I am he who searches hearts and minds, and I will repay each of you according to your deeds" (Revelation 2:23).

Words will be judged. "Everyone will have to give account on the day of judgment for every empty word they have spoken" (Matthew 12:36).

Believers' salvation is secure. "If [anyone's work] is burned up, the builder will suffer loss but yet will be saved—even though as one escaping through the flames" (1 Corinthians 3:15).

Christians should seek to run the race well so they can obtain the prize (1 Corinthians 9:24-25).

Biblical Pictures of Heaven

Description	Scripture	Meaning
A heavenly country	Hebrews 11:13-16	A country full of light, glory, splendor, and love
The Holy City	Revelation 21:1-2	A city of purity, with no sin
A home of righteousness	2 Peter 3:13	A perfect environment of righteousness
The kingdom of light	Colossians 1:12	A kingdom of Christ, who is the light of the world (John 8:12)
The paradise of God	Revelation 2:7	A paradise of pleasure. "Paradise" means "garden of delight."
The new Jerusalem	Revelation 21:10-14	This will be the capital city of heaven.

The Blessings of Heaven

No more death	"Death has been swallowed up in victory" (1 Corinthians 15:54).
No more pain	"There will no longer be any mourning, or crying, or pain " (Revelation 21:4 NASB).
No more Satan	"The devil, who deceived them, was thrown into the lake of burning sulfur" (Revelation 20:10).
Intimate fellowship with God	"Look! God's dwelling place is now among the people, and he will dwell with them. They will be his people" (Revelation 21:3).
Reunion with Christian loved ones	"The dead in Christ will rise first. After that, we who are still alive and are left will be caught up together with them in the clouds to meet the Lord in the air. And so we will be with the Lord forever" (1 Thessalonians 4:16-17).
Satisfaction of all needs	"They will hunger no longer, nor thirst anymore…God will wipe away every tear from their eyes" (Revelation 7:16-17 NASB).
Serene rest	"Blessed are the dead who die in the Lord from now on…They will rest from their labor" (Revelation 14:13).

Genesis and Revelation: Comparisons and Contrasts

Genesis	Revelation
Heaven and earth are created (Genesis 1:1–2:3).	A new heaven and earth appear (Revelation 21:1).
Day and night cycle continually (Genesis 1:5).	There is no more night (Revelation 21:25; 22:5).
Satan is on the loose (Genesis 3:15).	Satan is imprisoned in the lake of fire (Revelation 20:10).
The curse is received (Genesis 3:17-19).	The curse is removed (Revelation 22:3).
Humans experience pain and sorrow (Genesis 3:16-19).	Pain and sorrow are removed (Revelation 21:4).
Death enters the creation (Genesis 3:19).	Death is removed (Revelation 20:14; 21:4).
Fallen humans are banned from God's presence (Genesis 3:24).	Redeemed humans are welcomed into God's presence (Revelation 21:3).
Fallen humanity is clothed (Genesis 3:21).	Redeemed humanity is clothed (Revelation 6:11; 7:9,14).
God hides His face from humanity (Genesis 4:14).	God dwells with humanity face-to-face (Revelation 22:4).

Biblical Pictures of Hell

Revelation 19:20	"The fiery lake of burning sulfur"
Matthew 18:8	"Eternal fire"
Matthew 25:41	"The eternal fire prepared for the devil and his angels"
Matthew 13:42	"The blazing furnace, where there will be weeping and gnashing of teeth"
Matthew 7:13	"Destruction"
2 Thessalonians 1:9	"Everlasting destruction"
Matthew 25:46	"Eternal punishment"
Luke 13:27	"Away from me, all you evildoers!" (See also 2 Thessalonians 1:9.)
Mark 9:48	"The worms that eat them do not die, and the fire is not quenched."
Revelation 14:11	"The smoke of their torment will rise for ever and ever. There will be no rest day or night."
2 Peter 2:4	"Chains of darkness"

12

Prayer and Sanctification

Components of Prayer	
Thanksgiving	"Enter his gates with thanksgiving" (Psalm 100:4; see also Ephesians 5:20; Colossians 3:15).
Praise	Praise for God should always be on our lips (Psalm 34:1). We should continually offer to God a sacrifice of praise (Hebrews 13:15; see also Psalm 103:1-5,20-22).
Worship	We should worship God with reverence and awe (Hebrews 12:28). We worship Him alone (Exodus 20:3-5; see also Psalm 95:6).
Confession	"Whoever conceals their sins does not prosper, but the one who confesses and renounces them finds mercy" (Proverbs 28:13; see also 1 John 1:9).
Requests	"Do not be anxious about anything, but in every situation, by prayer and petition, with thanksgiving, present your requests to God" (Philippians 4:6).

Elements of Effective Prayer

God's will	"This is the confidence we have in approaching God: that if we ask anything according to his will, he hears us" (1 John 5:14).
Frequency	"Pray continually" (1 Thessalonians 5:17).
Purity	"If I had cherished sin in my heart, the Lord would not have listened" (Psalm 66:18).
Righteousness	"The LORD is far from the wicked, but he hears the prayer of the righteous" (Proverbs 15:29).
Persistence	"Ask and it will be given to you; seek and you will find; knock and the door will be opened to you" (Matthew 7:7). Or more literally, "*Ask and keep on asking...*"
Faith	"If anyone...does not doubt in their heart but believes...it will be done for them" (Mark 11:22-24).
Jesus' name	"I will do whatever you ask in my name... You may ask me for anything in my name, and I will do it" (John 14:13-14).
Trust	If your prayer seems unanswered, keep trusting God. He has a reason for the delay or for saying no (see 2 Corinthians 12:8-10).

What Can God Do When We Pray?

Enlighten the eyes of our hearts (Ephesians 1:18-19)

Fill us with the knowledge of His will (Colossians 1:9-12)

Make our love for other people increase and overflow (1 Thessalonians 3:10-13)

Encourage our hearts and strengthen us in every good deed and word (2 Thessalonians 2:16-17)

Protect us from harm and pain (1 Chronicles 4:10)

Deliver us from our troubles (Psalm 34:15-22)

Keep us from succumbing to lies and falsehood (Proverbs 30:7-9)

Provide the things we need (Matthew 6:11)

Help us to live righteously and blamelessly (1 Thessalonians 5:23)

Heal us when we are sick (James 5:14-15)

Three Aspects of Sanctification

The word "sanctification" means "to set apart." It indicates separation *from* sin and separation *to* a life of obedience to God.

Positional Sanctification
This becomes a reality for the believing sinner from the moment of conversion (1 Corinthians 6:11; Hebrews 10:10,14,29). The believer is positionally set apart from sin (Romans 1:7; 1 Corinthians 1:2).

Progressive Sanctification
This has to do with the believer's daily growth in grace, becoming in practice more and more set apart for God's use. This comes about by daily yielding to God and by keeping separate from sin (1 Peter 1:16).

Ultimate Sanctification
This is attained only when we are completely set apart from sin in heaven (following death). Believers will be like Christ (1 John 3:2) and conformed to His image (Romans 8:29).

Solomon's Advice on Life

Relationship with God	Proverbs 2:7-8; 3:5-6; 10:3,22,27; 14:26,31; 16:2,7; 17:3,5; 19:23; 20:27; 22:2; 28:25
Family	Proverbs 10:5; 13:24; 14:26; 15:20; 18:22; 19:14,18; 20:7; 22:6,15; 23:13-14; 27:15-16; 28:7; 30:17; 31:10-31
Friends	Proverbs 3:27-28; 12:26; 17:9,14,17; 18:24; 19:11; 20:3; 22:11; 25:17; 27:9-10
People to avoid	Proverbs 15:18; 16:28; 18:1; 20:19; 22:24-25; 23:6-8; 25:19-20; 26:18-21
Purity	Proverbs 5:3,7-14; 6:25-26,30-35; 7:6-27
Humility	Proverbs 3:7; 16:18; 18:12; 22:4; 25:27; 26:12; 27:2
Work	Proverbs 6:6-9; 10:26; 15:19; 20:4; 21:25; 22:13; 24:30-34; 26:16
Speech	Proverbs 10:19; 12:25; 16:24; 17:9,27; 18:8,13; 24:26; 25:11; 28:23; 29:5; 31:8-9
Money	Proverbs 8:18,21; 10:4,22; 11:1,4,24-25; 13:11; 14:23,31; 19:17; 20:13,17; 21:5,17; 22:7,9,26-27; 23:21; 28:19,22,25,27

13

Christian Ethics

The Ten Commandments

Commandments pertaining to the Israelites' relationship with God	1. Have no other gods.
	2. Have no graven images of God.
	3. Do not take the Lord's name in vain.
	4. Keep the Sabbath.
Commandments pertaining to the Israelites' relationships with each other	5. Honor your parents.
	6. Do not kill.
	7. Do not commit adultery.
	8. Do not steal.
	9. Do not bear false witness.
	10. Do not covet.

Jesus' Summation of the Law

"'Love the Lord your God with all your heart and with all your soul and with all your mind…Love your neighbor as yourself.' All the Law and the Prophets hang on these two commandments" (Matthew 22:37-40).

Drinking

Drunkenness is prohibited.	"Do not get drunk with wine, for that is debauchery, but be filled with the Spirit" (Ephesians 5:18).
Drinking in moderation is allowed.	"Stop drinking only water, and use a little wine because of your stomach and your frequent illnesses" (1 Timothy 5:23).
Not all things are helpful.	"All things are lawful for me, but not all things are profitable" (1 Corinthians 6:12 NASB).
Don't cause a brother to stumble.	"It is better not to eat meat or drink wine or do anything else that causes someone else to stumble" (Romans 14:21).
Consider the interests of others.	"Let each of you look not only to his own interests, but also to the interests of others" (Philippians 2:4 ESV).
Glorify God in all things.	"Whether you eat or drink, or whatever you do, do all to the glory of God" (1 Corinthians 10:31).

Sexual Sin

Marital sex	God created sex, and "everything created by God is good" (1 Timothy 4:4). But it is good only within the confines of the (male–female) marriage relationship (1 Corinthians 6:16; Ephesians 5:31; Hebrews 13:4).
Fornication	Christians are commanded to abstain from fornication (Acts 15:20). Paul affirmed that the body is not for fornication and that a man should flee it (1 Corinthians 6:13,18).
Adultery	"You shall not commit adultery" (Exodus 20:14). Even the thought of adultery is wrong (Matthew 5:27-28). Paul called adultery an evil work of the flesh (Galatians 5:19). "The sexually immoral...will be in the lake that burns with fire" (Revelation 21:8).
Temples of the Holy Spirit	The body is the temple of the Holy Spirit (1 Corinthians 6:19), so there should never be sexual sin.

Polygamy

God's prohibition	Scripture warns against multiple wives (Deuteronomy 17:17) and violating monogamy (1 Corinthians 7:2).
God's standard	From the very beginning God set the pattern by creating a monogamous marriage (Genesis 2:21-25).
The general practice of humanity	Monogamy was the general practice of the human race (Genesis 4:1) until interrupted by sin (Genesis 4:23).
Jesus' teaching	Our Lord affirmed God's original intention by creating one male and one female and joining them in marriage (Matthew 19:4).
Paul's teaching	"Each man should have sexual relations with his own wife, and each woman with her own husband" (1 Corinthians 7:2).
The example of Christ and the church	Monogamous marriage depicts the relationship between Christ and His bride, the church (Ephesians 5:31-32).

The Activist View of War

God empowered human government to take human life in cases where unruly people shed innocent blood (see Romans 13:1-7).

"Be subject to rulers and authorities, to be obedient, to be ready to do whatever is good" (Titus 3:1).

"Submit yourselves for the Lord's sake to every authority: whether to the emperor, as the supreme authority, or to governors, who are sent by him to punish those who do wrong and to commend those who do right" (1 Peter 2:13-14).

Jesus acknowledged God's ordaining of government when He said to Pilate, "You would have no power over me if it were not given to you from above" (John 19:11).

Conclusion
There is a connection between obedience to government and obedience to God. If one's government issues the command to go to war, one must obey the government as an expression of one's underlying obedience to God.

The Pacifist View of War

"Turn...the other cheek" (Matthew 5:38-42).

"Do not resist an evil person" (Matthew 5:39).

"Love your enemies, do good to them" (Luke 6:35; see also Matthew 5:44).

Jesus said the kingdom of God is not advanced by physical force (John 18:36).

Jesus stopped Peter from using a sword at Jesus' arrest (Matthew 26:52-54).

"You shall not murder" (Exodus 20:13).

The apostle Paul urged, "If possible, as far as it depends on you, live at peace with everyone" (Romans 12:18).

Vengeance belongs to God, so Christians should never retaliate (Romans 12:19).

We are instructed to not be overcome by evil but rather overcome evil by good (Romans 12:20-21).

Conclusion
Christians ought not participate in any war.

The Selectivist View of War

Being at peace with all	Paul urged Christians to be at peace with all people if possible (Romans 12:18), but it is not always possible.
Overcoming evil by good	Paul said Christians are to overcome evil with good (Romans 12:21), but this sometimes necessitates good and just people using force against evil.
Loving our enemies	We are to love our enemies as persons (Luke 6:35), but this does not mean we should love the evil things they do.
Turning the other cheek	"Turn the other cheek" (Matthew 5:38-42) does not apply to all circumstances. Christ was teaching not to return an insult for an insult.
Prohibition against killing	Scripture distinguishes murder (Exodus 20:13) from life-taking (Genesis 9:6). God permits government to take a life as a just deterrent to evil (Romans 13:1-4).
No unjust wars	Some wars are unjust. One ought not participate in these.

Conclusion
Christians ought to be selective, participating only in just wars.

The Principles of a Just War

Just cause	Defending a country is a just cause. Unprovoked aggression is not.
Just intention	War is not for revenge or conquest. Just wars are fought to rescue those who have been attacked or oppressed.
Last resort	War is to be entered into only after exhausting all methods of solving disputes nonviolently.
Formal declaration of war	Terrorists, militias, mercenaries, and angry mobs cannot declare war. Only legal government officials who are in power can declare war.
Limited objectives	The war should not aim at the complete destruction of the opposing nation. Hostilities should cease when objectives have been reached.
Proportionate means	Only the level of force necessary to secure victory over opposing combatants should be utilized.
Civilian immunity	The civilian population of a country should be immune from attack.

14

Apologetics

The Seven Major Worldviews

Worldview	Definition	Examples
Atheism	God does not exist.	Naturalism, humanism
Pantheism	God is all and all is God.	New Age teaching, Hinduism
Panentheism	God is in all and all is in God.	Process theology, some New Age teaching
Deism	God exists but is uninvolved with His creation.	Prevalent during Enlightenment times
Finite Godism	God exists but has certain limitations. For example, He may not be omniscient or omnipotent.	Openness theology
Polytheism	There are many gods.	Mormonism, Wicca
Monotheism	There is one true God.	Christianity, Judaism, Islam

Examples of Self-Defeating Arguments

When Someone Claims...	We Can Respond...
There are no absolutes.	Are you absolutely sure about that?
We cannot be certain about anything.	Are you certain about that?
We should doubt everything.	Should that statement be doubted?
We cannot know truth.	How do you know that is true?
We should never judge.	Is that your judgment?
It is true for you but not for me.	Is that statement true for you but not for me?
Truth about God is not objective.	Is that an objective truth about God?
Words cannot express meaning.	Do those words express meaning?
We must avoid making any confessional or creedal statements.	Isn't that a confessional or creedal statement?
There is no rational support for what we believe.	Is there any rational support for that belief?

Alleged Bible Contradictions

The following ten principles help us to resolve alleged Bible contradictions.

Something that is not explained is not necessarily unexplainable.

Partial reports are not necessarily false reports.

Divergent accounts are not necessarily false accounts.

Errors in manuscript copies do not necessarily point to errors in the original documents.

Consulting the context clears up most alleged contradictions.

Doctrines should not be based on obscure passages.

Clear verses interpret difficult verses.

The New Testament interprets the Old Testament.

The Bible does not approve of all it records (such as the words of Satan).

Each of the literary genres in Scripture has its own rules of interpretation.

Extrabiblical Christian Evidence

Many extrabiblical Christian sources that date between AD 95 and 170 affirm that Matthew, Mark, Luke, and John contain the actual words of Christ.

Clement, a church elder in Rome, cited portions of Matthew, Mark, and Luke as the words of Jesus.

Papias, the author of *Exposition of Oracles of the Lord*, cites the Gospels of Matthew, Mark, Luke, and John, presumably as canonical.

Justin Martyr, an apologist, considered all four Gospels to be Scripture.

The Didache, an ancient manual of Christianity from the end of the first century, cites portions of the three synoptic Gospels and refers to them as the words of Jesus.

Polycarp, a disciple of the apostle John, quotes portions of Matthew, Mark, and Luke as the words of Jesus.

Irenaeus, a disciple of Polycarp, quotes from 23 of the 27 New Testament books.

Extrabiblical Non-Christian Evidence

Significant non-Christian extrabiblical sources mention various aspects of Jesus' life and ministry.

Josephus, a Jewish historian born in AD 37, wrote *The Antiquities*, which clearly corroborates that Jesus was the leader of Christians, He had a brother named James, He did wonderful works, and He died by crucifixion.

The Talmud, a collection of ancient rabbinic writings that is hostile to Jesus, claims He was crucified on the eve of the Passover, He was involved in sorcery (an attempt to explain away His miracles), and Mary was an adulteress (an attempt to deny the virgin birth).

Pliny the Younger (AD 62–113), a Roman governor, wrote that Christians "sang in alternate verses a hymn to Christ, as to a god, and bound themselves by a solemn oath, not to any wicked deeds, but never to commit any fraud, theft, or adultery, never to falsify their word."

Tacitus, a Roman historian (AD 56–117), referred to Christians and to Christus, who "suffered the extreme penalty" (crucifixion) and who was the subject of "a most mischievous superstition" (an attempt to explain away the resurrection).

Taken together, extrabiblical non-Christian sources affirm that...

- Jesus lived during the time of Tiberius Caesar.
- He lived a virtuous life.
- He was a wonder-worker.
- He had a brother named James.
- He was acclaimed to be the Messiah.
- He was crucified under Pontius Pilate.
- He was crucified on the eve of the Passover.
- Darkness and an earthquake occurred when He died.
- His disciples believed He rose from the dead.
- His disciples were willing to die for their belief.
- His disciples denied the Roman gods and worshipped Jesus as God.

The Significance of Archaeology

Definition

"Archaeology" comes from two Greek words: *archaios* ("ancient things"), and *logos* ("study of").

A Science

Archaeology is categorized as a science because...

- Knowledge is acquired by systematic observation of discovered items.

- These items are classified and cataloged into an organized body of information.

- Assistance is sought from other sciences, such as anthropology.

Significance

- Biblical archaeology helps us to better understand the historical context of the Bible.

- It illuminates the meaning of some passages of Scripture.

- It verifies the accuracy and reliability of biblical teachings about numerous ancient customs, places, names, and events.

Old Testament Archaeological Discoveries

Creation	Many creation accounts have been discovered around the world.
The flood	Many pagan accounts of a universal flood have been discovered.
Sodom and Gomorrah	An excavation of Bab edh-Dhra, located near the Dead Sea in Wadi Araba, reveals extensive destruction by fire.
Egyptian hieroglyphics	The discovery of the Rosetta Stone at Rashid has helped scholars unlock Egypt's writing system.
Canaanite deities	Clay tablets at ancient Ugarit shed light on idolatry among pagans in Old Testament times.
Hittites	Information on the Hittites was discovered on 10,000 clay tablets at a ruin in Boghaz-Koy.
David and Solomon	Massive archaeological evidence has been discovered regarding David and Solomon.
Babylon	The ruins of ancient Babylon have been extensively excavated in modern Iraq.
Susa, Queen Esther's city	Susa, the ancient city of Queen Esther, has been excavated in modern Iran.

New Testament
Archaeological Discoveries

Nazareth	Artifacts from the time of Christ have been discovered in Nazareth (see Matthew 2:23; 4:13).
Bethsaida	Bethsaida, the birthplace of Peter, Andrew, and Philip, has been excavated.
Cana	The ruins at Khirbet Qana are apparently the biblical Cana, the city where Jesus turned water into wine (John 2:1-11).
Jacob's well	Jacob's well, where Jesus spoke with a Samaritan woman, has been discovered near Mount Gerizim.
Herod the Great	The ruins of Herod the Great's winter palace have been excavated at Jericho.
Pool of Bethesda	The pool of Bethesda, where Jesus healed a paralyzed man (John 5:2-11), has been excavated.
Synagogue in Capernaum	A synagogue in Capernaum has been discovered at the site of Tell Hum (see Matthew 4:13; Mark 1:21).
Pool of Siloam	The pool of Siloam, referenced in John 9, has been discovered.
Lazarus' tomb	Bethany, where Jesus raised Lazarus from the dead (John 11), has been located.

Pontius Pilate	A stone slab found at the ruins of Caesarea Maritima bears the words, "Pontius Pilate, Prefect of Judea."
Caiaphas	The ossuary of Caiaphas, the Jewish high priest who officiated at Jesus' trial, has been discovered (see Matthew 26:57; John 18:13-14).
Jesus' half brother	A limestone box has been discovered that bears the words "James, son of Joseph, brother of Jesus."
Jesus' tomb	Two tombs have been discovered in Jerusalem that may be the site from which Jesus was resurrected.
Damascus	Excavations have uncovered the remains of Straight Street, where Saul once stayed (Acts 9:11).
Book of Acts	Some 84 facts in the last 16 chapters of Acts have been archaeologically verified.
Titus and the temple	In the Arch of Titus in the ancient Roman forum is a scene in which Roman soldiers are portrayed carrying sacred items looted from the temple in Jerusalem in AD 70.

Ten Keys to Witnessing to Cult Members

1. Know basic Bible teachings.	No one can know all the false teachings of all the cults, but you can learn the Bible well enough to recognize false doctrine.
2. Don't assume every cultist believes the same thing.	Ask cultists what they believe rather than telling them what they believe. Not all cultists believe everything their groups teach.
3. Recognize that cultists are trained to answer objections.	Cultists seem to have an answer for everything. Don't get frustrated. Keep taking the discussion back to the Bible.
4. Check Scriptures.	Cultists invariably cite Scripture passages out of context. Always look the verses up and read them in context.
5. Define your terms.	Cultists use many of the same terms we do, such as God, Jesus, Holy Spirit, and salvation. However, they pour cultic meanings into these words. This means you need to define your terms.
6. Ask strategic questions.	By doing so, you can get them to think critically.
7. Always be loving.	Cultists don't care about how much you know until they know how much you care.